Table of Contents

Grading Options for This Course 3
Using This Teacher Guide 4
Course Objectives 4
Course Description 4
Suggested Daily Schedule 5
Worksheets for *The New Answers Book, Vol. 1* 13
Worksheets for *The New Answers Book, Vol. 2* 73
Practical Tests 141
Semester Tests 161
Answer Keys 171

Grading Options for This Course

It is always the prerogative of a parent/educator to assess student grades however he or she might deem best. The following is only a suggested guideline based on the material presented through this course:

1. Worksheets within the course are worth 100 points each.
2. Practical tests and review tests within the course are worth 100 points each.
3. A comprehensive exam can be created by a parent/educator by duplicating several quizzes more than once, if desired or required by state law.

To calculate the percentage of the worksheets and tests, the parent/educator may use the following guide. Divide total number of questions correct (example: 43) by the total number of questions possible (example: 46) to calculate the percentage out of 100 possible. 43/46 = 93 percent correct.

The suggested grade values are noted as follows: 90 to 100 percent = A; 80 to 89 percent = B; 70 to 79 percent = C; 60 to 69 percent = D; and 0 to 59 percent = F.

Special Note To Parents: Chapter 15 in *The New Answers Book Vol. 2* deals with the issue of gay marriage. You may want to review this chapter to make sure the material is age-appropriate for the maturity level of the student taking this course.

About the Authors

Ken Ham, founder and president of Answers in Genesis, joins with a group of popular and credentialed contributors that include Dr. Andrew Snelling (PhD in geology), Dr. Jason Lisle (PhD in astrophysics), Dr. Elizabeth Mitchell (MD), Dr. Danny Faulkner (MA in physics, and an MA and PhD in astronomy), Dr. David Menton (PhD in cell biology), Dr. Terry Mortenson (MDiv in systemic theology), Dr. Georgia Purdom (PhD in molecular genetics), Dr. A.J. Monty White (BS in chemistry, PhD), Dr. John Whitmore (PhD in biology), Dr. Tommy Mitchell (BA in cell biology, MD), and other scientists and apologetics scholars in a collection of questions and answers designed to provide fundamental insight and perspectives on topics related to science and religion.

Using This Teacher Guide

Features: The suggested weekly schedule enclosed has easy-to-manage lessons that guide the reading, worksheets, and all assessments. The pages of this guide are perforated and three-hole punched so materials are easy to tear out, hand out, grade, and store. Teachers are encouraged to adjust the schedule and materials needed in order to best work within their unique educational program.

Lesson Scheduling: Students are instructed to read the pages in their book and then complete the corresponding section provided by the teacher. Assessments that may include worksheets, activities, quizzes, and tests are given at regular intervals with space to record each grade. Space is provided on the weekly schedule for assignment dates, and flexibility in scheduling is encouraged. Teachers may adapt the scheduled days per each unique student situation. As the student completes each assignment, this can be marked with an "X" in the box.

🕐	Approximately 30 to 45 minutes per lesson, four days a week
🔑	Includes answer keys for worksheets and tests
📝	Worksheets for each chapter
📋	Tests are included to help reinforce learning and provide assessment opportunities
↻	Designed for grades 9 to 12 in a one-year course to earn 1 apologetics credit

Course Objectives: Students completing this course will

- Investigate some of the most popular cultural questions about science and Bible
- Explore how to think logically and apply biblical knowledge correctly
- Identify insights to the arguments brought against the faith and the solutions from the Bible and observational science
- Learn answers, information, and strategies when facing destructive influences found in the workplace or school environments
- Study fossils, the age of the earth, the beginning of life, and more in these two volumes focused on points of contention related to the Bible, faith, and science

Course Description: This curriculum has been put together to provide the answers to many common objections to biblical worldviews and scriptural authority of the Bible. Practical tests are included to strengthen the student's grasp of key concepts and terms, while providing critical thinking opportunities to put their knowledge to work. Students will learn to apply the biblical worldview to subjects such as evolution, carbon dating, Noah's ark and the Flood, and dozens more. They will discover answers to help know the depths of God's wisdom found in His Word and in His world, and why this matters to your life, your family, and your faith.

First Semester Suggested Daily Schedule

Date	Day	Assignment	Due Date	✓	Grade
		First Semester–First Quarter			
Week 1	Day 1	Glossary • Read Pages 355–365 • *New Answers Book; Vol. 1* • (NAB1)			
	Day 2	**New Answers Book 1: Glossary Worksheet 1** • Pages 15-16 Teacher Guide Lesson Planner • (TG)			
	Day 3	Ch 1: Is There Really a God? • Read Pages 7–24 • (NAB1)			
	Day 4	**New Answers Book 1: Ch 1 Worksheet 1** • Pages 17-18 • (TG)			
	Day 5				
Week 2	Day 6	Ch 2: Why Shouldn't Christians Accept Millions of Years? Read Pages 25–30 • (NAB1)			
	Day 7	**New Answers Book 1: Ch 2 Worksheet 1** • Pages 19-20 • (TG)			
	Day 8	Ch 3: Couldn't God Have Used Evolution? • Read Pages 31–38 (NAB1)			
	Day 9	**New Answers Book 1: Ch 3 Worksheet 1** • Pages 21-22 • (TG)			
	Day 10				
Week 3	Day 11	Ch 4: Don't Creationists Deny the Laws of Nature? Read Pages 39–46 • (NAB1)			
	Day 12	**New Answers Book 1: Ch 4 Worksheet 1** • Pages 23-24 • (TG)			
	Day 13	Ch 5: What About the Gap & Ruin-Reconstruction Theories? Read Pages 47–55 • (NAB1)			
	Day 14	Ch 5: What About the Gap & Ruin-Reconstruction Theories? Read Pages 56–63 • (NAB1)			
	Day 15				
Week 4	Day 16	**New Answers Book 1: Ch 5 Worksheet 1** • Pages 25-26 • (TG)			
	Day 17	Ch 6: Cain's Wife—Who Was She? • Read Pages 64–76 • (NAB1)			
	Day 18	**New Answers Book 1: Ch 6 Worksheet 1** • Pages 27-28 • (TG)			
	Day 19	**Practical Faith Test 1** • Pages 143-146 • (TG)			
	Day 20				
Week 5	Day 21	Ch 7: Doesn't Carbon-14 Dating Disprove the Bible? Read Pages 77–87 • (NAB1)			
	Day 22	**New Answers Book 1: Ch 7 Worksheet 1** • Pages 29-30 • (TG)			
	Day 23	Ch 8: Could God Really Have Created Everything in Six Days? Read Pages 88–100 • (NAB1)			
	Day 24	Ch 8: Could God Really Have Created Everything in Six Days? Read Pages 101–112 • (NAB1)			
	Day 25				
Week 6	Day 26	**New Answers Book 1: Ch 8 Worksheet 1** • Pages 31-32 • (TG)			
	Day 27	Ch 9: Does Radiometric Dating Prove the Earth is Old? Read Pages 113–124 • (NAB1)			
	Day 28	**New Answers Book 1: Ch 9 Worksheet 1** • Pages 33-34 • (TG)			
	Day 29	Ch 10: Was There Really a Noah's Ark & Flood? Read Pages 125–132 • (NAB1)			
	Day 30				

Date	Day	Assignment	Due Date	✓	Grade
Week 7	Day 31	Ch 10: Was There Really a Noah's Ark & Flood? Read Pages 133–140 • (NAB1)			
	Day 32	**New Answers Book 1: Ch 10 Worksheet 1** • Pages 35-36 • (TG)			
	Day 33	Ch 11: How Did Animals Spread All Over the World from Where the Ark Landed? • Read Pages 141–148 • (NAB1)			
	Day 34	**New Answers Book 1: Ch 11 Worksheet 1** • Pages 37-38 • (TG)			
	Day 35				
Week 8	Day 36	Ch 12: What Really Happened to the Dinosaurs? Read Pages 149–160 • (NAB1)			
	Day 37	Ch 12: What Really Happened to the Dinosaurs? Read Pages 161–169 • (NAB1)			
	Day 38	Ch 12: What Really Happened to the Dinosaurs? Read Pages 170–176 • (NAB1)			
	Day 39	**New Answers Book 1: Ch 12 Worksheet 1** • Pages 39-40 • (TG)			
	Day 40				
Week 9	Day 41	**Practical Faith Test 2** • Pages 147-148 • (TG)			
	Day 42	Ch 13: Why Don't We Find Human & Dinosaur Fossils Together? • Read Pages 178–185 • (NAB1)			
	Day 43	**New Answers Book 1: Ch 13 Worksheet 1** • Pages 41-42 • (TG)			
	Day 44	Ch 14: Can Catastrophic Plate Tectonics Explain Flood Geology? Read Pages 186–197 • (NAB1)			
	Day 45				
		First Semester–Second Quarter			
Week 1	Day 46	**New Answers Book 1: Ch 14 Worksheet 1** • Pages 43-44 • (TG)			
	Day 47	Ch 15: Don't Creationists Believe Some "Wacky" Things? Read Pages 198–206 • (NAB1)			
	Day 48	**New Answers Book 1: Ch 15 Worksheet 1** • Pages 45-46 • (TG)			
	Day 49	Ch 16: Where Does the Ice Age Fit? • Read Pages 207–219 (NAB1)			
	Day 50				
Week 2	Day 51	**New Answers Book 1: Ch 16 Worksheet 1** • Pages 47-48 • (TG)			
	Day 52	Ch 17: Are There Really Different Races? • Read Pages 220–227 (NAB1)			
	Day 53	Ch 17: Are There Really Different Races? • Read Pages 228–236 (NAB1)			
	Day 54	**New Answers Book 1: Ch 17 Worksheet 1** • Pages 49-50 • (TG)			
	Day 55				
Week 3	Day 56	Ch 18: Are ETs & UFOs Real? • Read Pages 237–244 (NAB1)			
	Day 57	**New Answers Book 1: Ch 18 Worksheet 1** • Pages 51-52 • (TG)			
	Day 58	Ch 19: Does Distant Starlight Prove the Universe is Old? Read Pages 245–254 (NAB1)			
	Day 59	**New Answers Book 1: Ch 19 Worksheet 1** • Pages 53-54 • (TG)			
	Day 60				

Date	Day	Assignment	Due Date	✓	Grade
Week 4	Day 61	**Practical Faith Test 3** • Pages 149-150 • (TG)			
	Day 62	Ch 20: Did Jesus Say He Created in Six Literal Days? Read Pages 255–258 (NAB1)			
	Day 63	**New Answers Book 1: Ch 20 Worksheet 1** • Pages 55-56 • (TG)			
	Day 64	Ch 21: How Did Defense/Attack Structures Come About? Read Pages 259–270 (NAB1)			
	Day 65				
Week 5	Day 66	**New Answers Book 1: Ch 21 Worksheet 1** • Pages 57-58 • (TG)			
	Day 67	Ch 22: Is Natural Selection the Same Thing as Evolution? Read Pages 271–282 • (NAB1)			
	Day 68	**New Answers Book 1: Ch 22 Worksheet 1** • Pages 59-60 • (TG)			
	Day 69	Ch 23: Hasn't Evolution Been Proven True? Read Pages 283–295 • (NAB1)			
	Day 70				
Week 6	Day 71	**New Answers Book 1: Ch 23 Worksheet 1** • Pages 61-62 • (TG)			
	Day 72	Ch 24: Did Dinosaurs Turn into Birds? • Read Pages 296–305 (NAB1)			
	Day 73	**New Answers Book 1: Ch 24 Worksheet 1** • Pages 63-64 • (TG)			
	Day 74	Ch 25: Does Archaeology Support the Bible? Read Pages 306–313 • (NAB1)			
	Day 75				
Week 7	Day 76	Ch 25: Does Archaeology Support the Bible? Read Pages 314–324 • (NAB1)			
	Day 77	**New Answers Book 1: Ch 25 Worksheet 1** • Pages 65-66 • (TG)			
	Day 78	**Practical Faith Test 4** • Pages 151-152 • (TG)			
	Day 79	Ch 26: Why Does God's Creation Include Death & Suffering? Read Pages 325–338 • (NAB1)			
	Day 80				
Week 8	Day 81	**New Answers Book 1: Ch 26 Worksheet 1** • Pages 67-68 • (TG)			
	Day 82	Ch 27: How Can I Use This Information to Witness? Read Pages 339–347 • (NAB1)			
	Day 83	**New Answers Book 1: Ch 27 Worksheet 1** • Pages 69-70 • (TG)			
	Day 84	Bonus Chapter: How Can We Use Dinosaurs to Spread the Creation Gospel Message? • Read Pages 348–353 • (NAB1)			
	Day 85				
Week 9	Day 86	**New Answers Book 1: Bonus Ch Worksheet 1** Page 71 • (TG)			
	Day 87	Review Worksheets for Chapters 1–15			
	Day 88	Review Worksheets for Chapters 16–27			
	Day 89	**New Answers Book 1: Semester Test 1** • Pages 163-166 • (TG)			
	Day 90				
		Mid-Term Grade			

Date	Day	Assignment	Due Date	✓	Grade
		Second Semester–Third Quarter			
Week 1	Day 91	Introduction: Why Is the Christian Worldview Collapsing in America? • Read Pages 9–14 • *New Answers Book; Vol. 2* • (NAB2)			
	Day 92	**New Answers Book 2: Introduction Worksheet 1** Pages 75-76 • Lesson Planner • (TG)			
	Day 93	Ch 1: What Is a Biblical Worldview? • Read Pages 15–21 (NAB2)			
	Day 94	**New Answers Book 2: Ch 1 Worksheet 1** • Pages 77–78 • (TG)			
	Day 95				
Week 2	Day 96	Ch 2: What's the Best "Proof" of Creation? Read Pages 23–32 • (NAB2)			
	Day 97	**New Answers Book 2: Ch 2 Worksheet 1** • Pages 79-80 • (TG)			
	Day 98	Ch 3: Are Biblical Creationists Divisive? Read Pages 33–39 • (NAB2)			
	Day 99	**New Answers Book 2: Ch 3 Worksheet 1** • Pages 81-82 • (TG)			
	Day 100				
Week 3	Day 101	Ch 4: How Old Is the Earth? • Read Pages 41–52 • (NAB2)			
	Day 102	**New Answers Book 2: Ch 4 Worksheet 1** • Pages 83–84 • (TG)			
	Day 103	Ch 5: Are There Gaps in the Genesis Geologies? Read Pages 53–62 • (NAB2)			
	Day 104	**New Answers Book 2: Ch 5 Worksheet 1** • Pages 85-86 • (TG)			
	Day 105				
Week 4	Day 106	Ch 6: Can Natural Processes Explain the Origin of Life? Read Pages 63–72 • (NAB2)			
	Day 107	**New Answers Book 2: Ch 6 Worksheet 1** • Pages 87-88 • (TG)			
	Day 108	Ch 7: Are Mutations Part of the "Engine" of Evolution? Read Pages 73–82 • (NAB2)			
	Day 109	**New Answers Book 2: Ch 7 Worksheet 1** • Pages 89-90 • (TG)			
	Day 110				
Week 5	Day 111	**Practical Faith Test 5** • Pages 153-154 • (TG)			
	Day 112	Ch 8: Did Humans Really Evolve from Apelike Creatures? Read Pages 83–93 • (NAB2)			
	Day 113	**New Answers Book 2: Ch 8 Worksheet 1** • Pages 91-92 • (TG)			
	Day 114	Ch 9: Does the Bible Say Anything about Astronomy? Read Pages 95–102 • (NAB2)			
	Day 115				
Week 6	Day 116	**New Answers Book 2: Ch 9 Worksheet 1** • Pages 93-94 • (TG)			
	Day 117	Ch 10: Does the Big Bang Fit with the Bible? Read Pages 103–110 • (NAB2)			
	Day 118	**New Answers Book 2: Ch 10 Worksheet 1** Pages 95-96 • (TG)			
	Day 119	Ch 11: Where Did the Idea of "Millions of Years" Come From? • Read Pages 111–121 • (NAB2)			
	Day 120				

Date	Day	Assignment	Due Date	✓	Grade
Week 7	Day 121	**New Answers Book 2: Ch 11 Worksheet 1** • Pages 97-98 • (TG)			
	Day 122	Ch 12: What's Wrong with Progressive Creation? Read Pages 123–133 • (NAB2)			
	Day 123	**New Answers Book 2: Ch 12 Worksheet 1** Pages 99-100 • (TG)			
	Day 124	Ch 13: Is the Intelligent Design Movement Christian? Read Pages 135–141 • (NAB2)			
	Day 125				
Week 8	Day 126	**New Answers Book 2: Ch 13 Worksheet 1** Pages 101-102 • (TG)			
	Day 127	Ch 14: Can Creationists Be "Real" Scientists? Read Pages 143–148 • (NAB2)			
	Day 128	**New Answers Book 2: Ch 14 Worksheet 1** Pages 103-104 • (TG)			
	Day 129	Ch 15: How Should a Christian Respond to "Gay Marriage"? Read Pages 149–158 • (NAB2)			
	Day 130				
Week 9	Day 131	**New Answers Book 2: Ch 15 Worksheet 1** Pages 105-106 • (TG)			
	Day 132	**Practical Faith Test 6** • Pages 155-156 • (TG)			
	Day 133	Ch 16: Did People like Adam and Noah Really Live Over 900 Years of Age? • Read Pages 159–167 • (NAB2)			
	Day 134	**New Answers Book 2: Ch 16 Worksheet 1** Pages 107-108 • (TG)			
	Day 135				
		Second Semester–Fourth Quarter			
Week 1	Day 136	Ch 17: Why 66? • Read Pages 169–178 • (NAB2)			
	Day 137	**New Answers Book 2: Ch 17 Worksheet 1** Pages 109-110 • (TG)			
	Day 138	Ch 18: What Was the Christmas Star? Read Pages 179–184 • (NAB2)			
	Day 139	**New Answers Book 2: Ch 18 Worksheet 1** Pages 111-112 • (TG)			
	Day 140				
Week 2	Day 141	Ch 19: Is Jesus God? • Read Pages 185–193 • (NAB2)			
	Day 142	**New Answers Book 2: Ch 19 Worksheet 1** Pages 113-114 • (TG)			
	Day 143	Ch 20: Information: Evidence for a Creator? Read Pages 195–206 • (NAB2)			
	Day 144	**New Answers Book 2: Ch 20 Worksheet 1** Pages 115-116 • (TG)			
	Day 145				

Date	Day	Assignment	Due Date	✓	Grade
Week 3	Day 146	Ch 21: Is Evolution a Religion? Read Pages 207–217 • (NAB2)			
	Day 147	**New Answers Book 2: Ch 21 Worksheet 1** Pages 117-118 • (TG)			
	Day 148	Ch 22: Is the Bible Enough? • Read Pages 219–228 • (NAB2)			
	Day 149	**New Answers Book 2: Ch 22 Worksheet 1** Pages 119-120 • (TG)			
	Day 150				
Week 4	Day 151	Ch 23: Aren't Millions of Years Required for Geological Processes? • Read Pages 229–244 • (NAB2)			
	Day 152	**New Answers Book 2: Ch 23 Worksheet 1** Pages 121-122 • (TG)			
	Day 153	**Practical Faith Test 7** • Pages 157-158 • (TG)			
	Day 154	Ch 24: Doesn't Egyptian Chronology Prove That the Bible Is Unreliable? • Read Pages 245–254 • (NAB2)			
	Day 155				
Week 5	Day 156	Ch 24: Doesn't Egyptian Chronology Prove That the Bible Is Unreliable? • Read Pages 255–263 • (NAB2)			
	Day 157	**New Answers Book 2: Ch 24 Worksheet 1** Pages 123-124 • (TG)			
	Day 158	Ch 25: What about Satan and the Origin of Evil? Read Pages 265–276 • (NAB2)			
	Day 159	**New Answers Book 2: Ch 25 Worksheet 1** Pages 125-126 • (TG)			
	Day 160				
Week 6	Day 161	Ch 26: Why Is the Scopes Trial Significant? Read Pages 277–282 • (NAB2)			
	Day 162	**New Answers Book 2: Ch 26 Worksheet 1** Pages 127-128 • (TG)			
	Day 163	Ch 27: Isn't the Bible Full of Contradictions? Read Pages 283–297 • (NAB2)			
	Day 164	**New Answers Book 2: Ch 27 Worksheet 1** Pages 129-130 • (TG)			
	Day 165				
Week 7	Day 166	Ch 28: Was the Dispersion at Babel a Real Event? Read Pages 299–311 • (NAB2)			
	Day 167	**New Answers Book 2: Ch 28 Worksheet 1** Pages 131-132 • (TG)			
	Day 168	Ch 29: When Does Life Begin? • Read Pages 313–323 • (NAB2)			
	Day 169	**New Answers Book 2: Ch 29 Worksheet 1** Pages 133-134 • (TG)			
	Day 170				

Date	Day	Assignment	Due Date	✓	Grade
Week 8	Day 171	Ch 30: Do Creationists Believe in "Weird" Physics like Relativity, Quantum Mechanics, and String Theory? Read Pages 325–339 • (NAB2)			
	Day 172	**New Answers Book 2: Ch 30 Worksheet 1** Pages 135-136 • (TG)			
	Day 173	Ch 31: Doesn't the Order of Fossils in the Rock Record Favor Long Ages? • Read Pages 341–354 • (NAB2)			
	Day 174	**New Answers Book 2: Ch 31 Worksheet 1** Pages 137-138 • (TG)			
	Day 175				
Week 9	Day 176	**Practical Faith Test 8** • Pages 159-160 • (TG)			
	Day 177	Conclusion: The Biggest Question of All Read Pages 355–359 • (NAB2) **New Answers Book 2: Conclusion Worksheet 1** Page 139 • (TG)			
	Day 178	Review Worksheets for Chapters 1–31			
	Day 179	**New Answers Book 2: Semester Test 2** • Pages 167-170 • (TG)			
	Day 180				
		Final Grade			

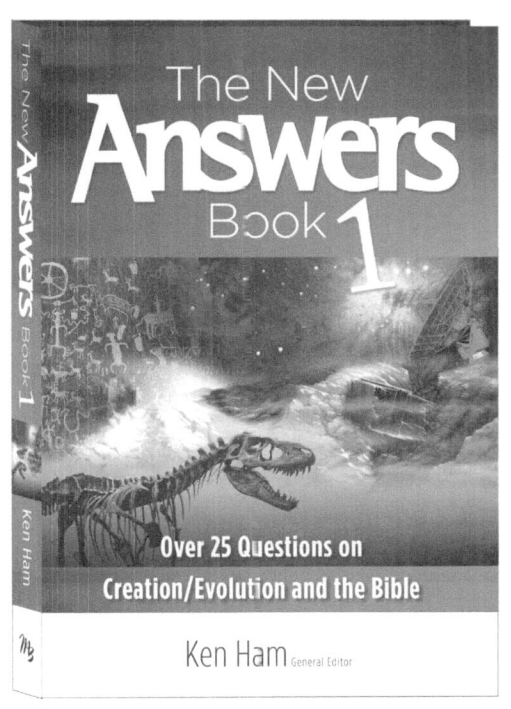

Cultural Issues Worksheets

for Use with

The New Answers Book 1

| The New Answers Book 1 | Glossary | Day 2 | Glossary Worksheet 1 | Name |

Questions

1. Is a theory widely held by a number of scientists or scholars the same thing as a fact? Explain why or why not, using the glossary definition for the word *theory*.

2. Explain the difference between operational (observational) science and historical (origins) science.

3. What is the difference between macroevolution and microevolution?

4. What is old earth creation? Give two specific examples of this concept from the glossary.
   a.

   b.

First Semester/First Quarter 15

5. Define the following words:
   a. exegesis -

   b. eisegesis -

   c. biblical creation model -

   d. big bang model -

6. What are the three aspects of the cell theory? Why does it create issues for evolutionists?

7. What is "compromise" in the context of studying the origins of life on Earth and Scripture? Give some examples related to the Book of Genesis.

| The New Answers Book 1 | Is There Really a God? | Day 4 | Chapter 1 Worksheet 1 | Name |

Questions

1. How does design point to an intelligent Creator God?

2. Both evolutionists and creationists agree that natural selection and mutations bring about change in an organism, but how do natural selection and mutations fall short in explaining design?

3. How does genetic information point to a Creator?

4. Why is a belief in God actually foundational to logical thought and scientific inquiry?

5. What is faith? What is the difference between faith in God and faith in evolution?

6. What is a difficulty some people have in accepting a Creator God?

| *The New Answers Book 1* | Why Shouldn't Christians Accept Millions of Years? | Day 7 | Chapter 2 Worksheet 1 | Name |

Questions

1. List six reasons why a six-day creation is vital to the Christian faith.

   a.

   b.

   c.

   d.

   e.

   f.

2. How did the idea of millions of years come about? Who developed this idea?

3. Discuss the evidences of a young earth listed in the chapter, and discuss why each is significant.

4. Write a short paragraph on the concept of the Bible being a history book — cite a couple of historical facts not already noted in the chapter (for example, ancient cities like Petra, ancient cultures like the Hittites, etc.).

5. Before starting this course, did you ever consider science an area of interest for someone interested in defending the Bible as truth as written? Why or why not?

| The New Answers Book 2 | Couldn't God Have Used Evolution? | Day 9 | Chapter 3 Worksheet 1 | Name |

Questions

1. How does the belief that God used evolution as His method of creation harm the gospel?

2. How does the belief that God used evolution as His method of creation harm the character of God?

3. The real issue behind saying that God used millions of years of evolution as His method of creation is that it puts the authority of God's Word against man's fallible opinion. How is this true?

4. How did evolutionist Thomas Huxley seem to understand the issue of compromising Scripture by introducing evolutionary ideas into the reading of it? How did he use this to undermine Christian views about the validity of Scripture?

5. Christian leader Charles Hodge is quoted in the book as having said, "The Church has been forced more than once to alter her interpretation of the Bible to accommodate the discoveries of science. But this has been done without doing any violence to the Scriptures or in any degree impairing their authority." What do you think of Hodge's opinion, and why is it relevant to current discussions regarding Scripture?

| The New Answers Book 1 | Don't Creationists Deny the Laws of Nature? | Day 12 | Chapter 4 Worksheet 1 | Name |

Questions

1. How do these laws of nature confirm the Bible's testimony and/or contradict evolutionary teaching?

   a. Law of biogenesis

   b. Laws of chemistry

   c. Laws of planetary motion

   d. Laws of physics

   e. Universal constants

f. The anthropic principle

g. Laws of mathematics

h. Laws of logic

i. Uniformity of nature

2. How are the laws of nature illogical within an atheistic worldview?

| *The New Answers Book 1* | What About the Gap & Ruin-Reconstruction Theories? | Day 16 | Chapter 5 Worksheet 1 | Name |

Questions

1. In general, what is the gap theory?

2. Specifically, what is the "ruin-reconstruction" version of the gap theory?

3. How is the gap theory different from and similar to the ideas of "theistic evolution" and "progressive creation"?

4. Borrow copies of the *Scofield Reference Bible*, *Dake's Annotated Reference Bible*, or *The Newberry Reference Bible* from your local pastor or local library. Research for yourself what these books say concerning the gap theory.

5. What is the main reason people adhere to positions such as the gap theory?

6. Research Western Bible commentaries, written before the 18th century. How did the writers of these commentaries view Genesis 1–11 as a whole, and Genesis 1:1–2 in particular?

7. How does the message of the gap theory undermine the message of the gospel?

8. List and describe three biblical reasons that the gap theory cannot be true.

9. List and describe three non-biblical ways in which the gap theory is inconsistent.

10. How are the words *bara* and *asah* used in the Old Testament? Why should these words be considered interchangeable?

11. How does the actual grammatical structure of Genesis 1:1–2 preclude a gap of time being inserted?

12. Why is it inappropriate to translate the Hebrew word *hayetah* as "became" in the context of Genesis 1:1–2?

13. How do those who accept the gap theory translate *tohu* and *bohu*?

14. How has the modern meaning of the word *replenish* been used to support the gap theory? Why is this inaccurate?

| | *The New Answers Book 1* | Cain's Wife — Who Was She? | Day 18 | Chapter 6 Worksheet 1 | Name |

Questions

1. Why is it important that Adam was the only man in the beginning?

2. Why is Jesus called the "Last Adam"?

3. Who was Cain's wife?

4. When was the Jewish law against intermarriage implemented? Why was it implemented?

5. What are some of the common objections to the concept of Cain's wife being a descendant of Adam?

6. Why is the idea that Cain married his wife in the Land of Nod incorrect?

7. What did you learn about the origins of technology from this chapter of the book?

| The New Answers Book 1 | Doesn't Carbon-14 Dating Disprove the Bible? | Day 22 | Chapter 7 Worksheet 1 | Name |

Questions

1. The carbon-dating method works on what types of substances?

2. Theoretically, how does carbon-dating work?

3. What is the critical assumption used in carbon-14 dating?

4. How would rejecting this assumption affect the outcome of one's experiments?

5. How could the global Flood have affected carbon-14 dating?

6. What findings did the recent RATE group record? How did they reach their conclusions?

7. What does carbon-14 dating prove about the age of the earth?

| The New Answers Book 1 | Could God Really Have Created Everything in Six Days? | Day 26 | Chapter 8 Worksheet 1 | Name |

Questions

1. What is the main reason some people believe Genesis 1 speaks of long ages?

2. Why is it inappropriate to refer to "nature" as the "67th book of the Bible"?

3. Why is it improper and unwise to use the findings of secular "origins" science to reinterpret Scripture?

4. Look up the word *day* in a Hebrew lexicon. Which Hebrew word refers to normal-length (approximately 24-hour) days? Long periods of time? (Note: There are Hebrew lexicons available online. For example: www.biblestudytools.com/lexicons/hebrew/.)

5. Which Hebrew word for day is used in Genesis 1?

6. Why is it important to consider the context when determining the meaning of a word?

7. Discuss and explain the eight objections to a literal, six-day creation and the answers to those objections.

8. How does the evolutionary order differ from the biblical order of creation? (See chart on page 110 of your textbook.)

9. What is theistic evolution? List some theological problems with accepting this view.

10. What is progressive creation? List some theological problems with accepting this view.

11. Why is it important to accept that the days mentioned in Genesis 1 are regular-length days?

| *The New Answers Book 1* | Does Radiometric Dating Prove the Earth Is Old? | Day 28 | Chapter 9 Worksheet 1 | Name |

Questions

1. Theoretically, how does radioisotope dating work?

2. What types of rocks are used with radioisotope dating?

3. Define half-life.

4. What critical assumptions are made in radioisotope dating?

5. How would rejecting these assumptions change the outcome of one's experiments?

6. Theoretically, how does isochron dating work?

7. How did the experiments done by the RATE group give evidence for a young earth?

| *The New Answers Book 1* | Was There Really a Noah's Ark & Flood? | Day 32 | Chapter 10 Worksheet 1 | Name |

Questions

1. How was Noah able to build such a large, seaworthy vessel?

2. According to the Bible, what kinds of animals did Noah have with him on the ark? What kinds of organisms were not on the ark?

3. How is a "created kind" defined? How many "kinds" of animals were necessary for Noah to take on the ark?

4. How did Noah care for all the animals on the ark?

5. For the more technically minded: How seaworthy was the ark?

6. According to the Bible, what were the two main sources of water for the global Flood of Noah's day?

7. Discuss the scriptural passages that show Noah's Flood was global.

8. Discuss the geological evidences that support a global Flood of Noah's day.

| | The New Answers Book 1 | How Did Animals Spread All Over the World from Where the Ark Landed? | Day 34 | Chapter 11 Worksheet 1 | Name |

Questions

1. According to the Bible, how did all the animals get to the ark?

2. Why do we not find fossils of kangaroos along the way from the ark to Australia?

3. How did the Ice Age affect post-Flood animal and human distribution over the earth?

4. Explain the claims of the Recolonization Theory, and discuss the errors of this theory.

5. Summarize in three paragraphs the main points that caught your attention from this chapter.

| The New Answers Book 1 | What Really Happened to the Dinosaurs? | Day 39 | Chapter 12 Worksheet 1 | Name |

Questions

1. In your own words, explain the history of dinosaurs according to evolutionists and according to the Bible.

2. Review the difference between origins science and operational science. Which aspects of paleontology fall under the realm of origins science? Which aspects are considered operational science?

3. Does the Bible mention dinosaurs? Where?

4. Discuss some evidences that show that dinosaur bones have not been around for millions of years.

5. Why is it important that we are able to explain the existence of dinosaurs within a biblical worldview?

| *The New Answers Book 1* | Why Don't We Find Human & Dinosaur Fossils Together? | Day 43 | Chapter 13 Worksheet 1 | Name |

Questions

1. When asking the question of why we don't find human and dinosaur fossils together, what other factors should be taken into account? Why are these factors significant?

2. Does the lack of human fossils buried with dinosaur fossils support the evolutionary idea that humans and dinosaurs did not live together? Why or why not?

3. Human fossils are found in layers that are considered to be what by creationists?

4. When compared to the other types of fossils, do dinosaur fossils make up very high or very low numbers of those found?

5. What is the Hebrew word that is translated as "blot out" or "destroy"?

6. In discussing why human fossils from the Flood have not been found, why is it important to consider the estimates of the population at the time, and the possible density of their numbers in different locations?

7. If human fossils were found in layers where dinosaur fossils are found, would that prove the creationists correct?

| The New Answers Book 1 | Can Catastrophic Plate Tectonics Explain Flood Geology? | Day 46 | Chapter 14 Worksheet 1 | Name |

Questions

1. In your own words, define *plate tectonics*.

2. What are the three types of horizontal movements of the earth's plates? What causes these movements?

3. Research the history of plate tectonics — how has it developed over the years?

4. How does observable evidence point to catastrophic movements of the earth's plates and not to slow-and-gradual movements?

5. What does the Bible say about catastrophic plate tectonics?

| The New Answers Book 1 | Don't Creationists Believe Some "Wacky" Things? | Day 48 | Chapter 15 Worksheet 1 | Name |

Questions

1. What "wacky" things have you, as a Christian, been accused of? How would you answer your accuser?

2. What two examples of biblical verses were noted in this chapter stating the earth was round?

3. How has the concept of a flat earth been used to try to discredit Christians in the past?

4. How can a mutation be considered beneficial and not beneficial at the same time in terms of a beetle losing its wings or sickle cell anemia in humans?

5. Does your status as a Christian depend on what you believe about the age of the earth?

6. Why does believing in long ages for the earth create an inconsistency for Christians?

| The New Answers Book 1 | Where Does the Ice Age Fit? | Day 51 | Chapter 16 Worksheet 1 | Name |

Questions

1. How would the global Flood of Noah's day have provided the proper conditions for the Ice Age?

2. What evidences are there that support an Ice Age?

3. Give a brief explanation of an evolutionist's views about ice ages.

4. How do we know the Ice Age occurred *after* the Flood?

5. How long did the Ice Age last?

6. List the possible biblical references to the Ice Age.

7. Discuss the answer to the question, "What happened to the woolly mammoths?"

8. How does the Lake Missoula flood help us understand the impact of the global Flood?

| The New Answers Book 1 | Are There Really Different Races? | Day 54 | Chapter 17 Worksheet 1 | Name |

Questions

1. How have evolutionary-based ideas provided support for racism?

2. Explain, in your own words, how the characteristics of various people groups have come about.

3. What is the biblical basis and purpose for marriage?

4. Read Genesis 9:18–27. Who received the curse pronounced by Noah? Why did Noah pronounce this curse? Is the black "race" the result of a curse on Ham? Explain your answer.

5. List some biblical examples of so-called "interracial marriages" and explain the significance of them.

6. What is the only kind of "interracial" marriage the Bible forbids?

| *The New Answers Book 1* | Are ETs & UFOs Real? | Day 57 | Chapter 18 Worksheet 1 | Name |

Questions

1. How does the idea of extraterrestrial life stem largely from a belief in evolution?

2. What theological problems arise for those who believe alien races exist?

3. What is the primary motivation behind searching for "life" elsewhere in the universe?

4. Why is it said that the earth is unique and designed by God for life but the "heaven's are the Lord's"?

5. Why is the question, "Where is everybody?" relevant to the question of extraterrestrials?

| The New Answers Book 1 | Does Distant Starlight Prove the Universe Is Old? | Day 59 | Chapter 19 Worksheet 1 | Name |

Questions

1. Discuss the implications of the idea that God created light "on its way" on day 4 of creation.

2. Discuss the assumptions that are involved in the light travel-time arguments. How does each affect the final result?

3. In your own words, explain the difference between universal time and local time.

4. Why is God not bound by the laws of nature?

5. What is the light travel-time problem present in the big-bang model?

6. What is inflation? Does this explanation satisfy the light travel-time problem of the big-bang model? Why or why not?

7. Answer the question posed in the chapter title.

| The New Answers Book 1 | Did Jesus Say He Created in Six Literal Days? | Day 63 | Chapter 20 Worksheet 1 | Name |

Questions

1. List and discuss the Old Testament and New Testament passages of Scripture in which Jesus states the young age of the earth.

2. What Old Testament accounts does Jesus treat as historical fact? What impact do Jesus' claims have?

3. Among the Jewish people, what was their understanding of how old the earth was in relation to Creation at the time of Jesus? How do we know this?

4. Theophanies are essentially defined as occurrences when a person actually sees a deity. In the context of Christianity, it refers to when God appeared to people in a way that one or more of their senses (sight, sound, etc.) could comprehend Him. Briefly explain this in context of what you learned in this chapter about Jesus.

5. What is the importance in understanding what Jesus said in a discussion of origins?

| The New Answers Book 1 | How Did Defense/Attack Structures Come About? | Day 66 | Chapter 21 Worksheet 1 | Name |

Questions

1. How does the idea that defense/attack structures were part of God's original design impact man's view of God and His character?

2. According to Genesis 3, is the world as we see it the same as it was in the beginning? If not, what changed the world?

3. List the passages of Scripture that address the changes in nature, and discuss each change.

4. What are the two primary alternatives that explain defense/attack structures from a biblical perspective?

5. Along with the Curse proclaimed in Genesis 3, what else did God promise? Why is this significant?

| The New Answers Book 1 | Is Natural Selection the Same Thing as Evolution? | Day 68 | Chapter 22 Worksheet 1 | Name |

Questions

1. What is the definition of *natural selection* from an evolutionist's perspective? From a creationist's perspective?

2. Who was one of the first to formulate the theory of natural selection? How was his theory different from Darwin's?

3. How did natural selection benefit animals in the post-Flood world?

4. Discuss the limitations of natural selection. How do these support biblical creation and not evolution?

5. Define *species*.

6. What has been observed about the formation of new species? How does this support a young earth?

| The New Answers Book 1 | Hasn't Evolution Been Proven True? | Day 71 | Chapter 23 Worksheet 1 | Name |

Questions

1. What is the significance of the differences between the creation order of events and the evolutionary order of events?

2. What is the problem with the cosmologists' claim that a vacuum can, under some circumstances, give rise to matter?

3. How did Miller's chemical experiment fail to fully produce life from non-life?

First Semester/Second Quarter // 61

4. What is "comparative anatomy"? What do the differences between such structures signify? What do the similarities prove about their Creator?

5. Did Darwin's observations about the differences in finch beaks on the Galapagos Islands help him prove his theory, or did they disprove his theory?

| The New Answers Book 1 | Did Dinosaurs Turn into Birds? | Day 73 | Chapter 24 Worksheet 1 | Name |

Questions

1. What are the differences between what the Bible says and what evolutionists claim about the origin of birds and the origin of dinosaurs?

2. What are the differences between the blood, hips, "hands," and lungs of birds and those of dinosaurs?

3. What fossil was touted by biology textbooks as the perfect transitional fossil? What has been proven about this fossil?

4. How can an ectothermic animal adjust its temperature?

5. Did feathered dinosaurs exist?

6. In the creation record from the Bible, which came first, dinosaurs or birds?

| The New Answers Book 1 | Does Archaeology Support the Bible? | Day 77 | Chapter 25 Worksheet 1 | Name |

Questions

1. What is the special role of the Bible regarding its relation between God and man?

NOTE: YOU CAN USE YOUR BOOK AS NEEDED IN ANSWERING THE FOLLOWING QUESTIONS.

2. Discuss the archaeological evidences that support the Bible's accuracy in Genesis 1–11.

3. Discuss the archaeological evidences that support the Bible's accuracy in Genesis 11–36.

4. Discuss the archaeological evidences that support the Bible's accuracy in Genesis 37–50.

5. Discuss the archaeological evidences that support the Bible's accuracy in Exodus to Deuteronomy.

6. Discuss the archaeological evidences that support the Bible's accuracy in dealing with the time of Joshua through the time of Saul.

7. Discuss the archaeological evidences that support the Bible's accuracy in dealing with the time of David through the time of Solomon.

8. Discuss the archaeological evidences that support the Bible's accuracy in dealing with the Assyrian Period.

9. Discuss the archaeological evidences that support the Bible's accuracy in dealing with the Babylonians and Nebuchadnezzar.

10. Discuss the archaeological evidences that support the Bible's accuracy in dealing with Cyrus and the Medes and Persians.

11. Discuss the archaeological evidences that support the Bible's accuracy in dealing with Ezra and Nehemiah.

12. Discuss the archaeological evidences that support the Bible's accuracy in dealing with the information in the Dead Sea Scrolls.

13. Discuss the archaeological evidences that support the Bible's accuracy in dealing with the person of our Lord.

14. Discuss the archaeological evidences that support the Bible's accuracy in dealing with the New Testament, the early church, and the early years of Christianity.

15. Why is the study of archaeology beneficial to Christians?

16. Discuss and memorize the acrostic that shows archaeology's relevance to the Bible.

| The New Answers Book 1 | Why Does God's Creation Include Death & Suffering? | Day 81 | Chapter 26 Worksheet 1 | Name |

Questions

1. In a Hebrew dictionary or online, look up the term *nephesh* and write its definitions. (Example: http://www.biblestudytools.com/lexicons/hebrew/.) How is the word used in Genesis 1?

2. What kinds of things have *nephesh* life?

3. Why did God's command to Adam and the animals to eat plants for food *not* involve death, in the biblical sense?

4. Why is there so much death and suffering in the world today?

5. How did sin impact the earth and mankind in the past? Today?

6. How does having an evolutionary foundation impact one's views on death and suffering? How does it impact man's hope for the future?

7. What hope is there for Christians who are struggling through physical trials?

| The New Answers Book 1 | How Can I Use This Information to Witness? | Day 83 | Chapter 27 Worksheet 1 | Name |

Questions

1. Describe someone who is typed as a "Jew" (according to the context of this chapter).

2. Describe someone who is typed as a "Greek" (according to the context of this chapter).

3. What did the Jews who lived around the time of Jesus already understand about creation, the Fall, sin, the law of Moses, and sacrifices?

4. How did Peter address these Jews in light of what they understood?

5. What did the Greeks who lived around the time of Jesus not understand about creation, the Fall, sin, the law of Moses, and sacrifices?

6. How did Paul address them in light of what they understood?

7. How have most modern nations of today changed from being like the Jews of old to the Greeks of old?

8. What is vital to a Christian's evangelism in today's Greek culture?

9. How can you use the information you have gained from this book?

|  | The New Answers Book 2 | How Can We Use Dinosaurs to Spread the Creation Gospel Message? | Day 86 | Bonus Chapter Worksheet 1 | Name |

Questions

The following exercise takes place in the context of two friends talking — one a Christian with a biblical worldview (you), and another who is not a Christian (Charles). Charles is making comments about dinosaurs and how they prove evolution is true and not the Bible. Your part of the dialogue (written or verbally presented) is to use the information you learned from this bonus chapter to help spread biblical truth as well as the gospel to Charles.

1.

Charles: Dinosaurs prove evolution is true. The Bible doesn't even mention dinosaurs!

You:

2.

Charles: Okay, then how do you explain all the dinosaur fossils from millions of years ago?

You:

3.

Charles: Dinosaurs happened long before man — how could they even fit within a biblical timeline?

You:

First Semester/Second Quarter // 71

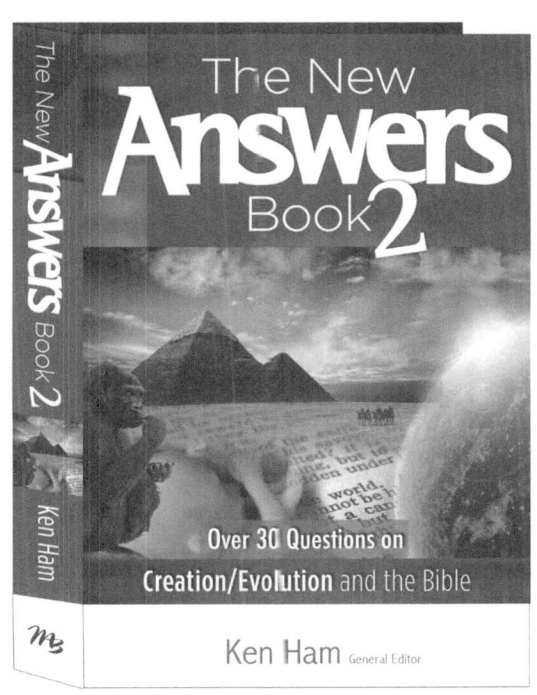

Cultral Issues Worksheets

for Use with

The New Answers Book 2

| The New Answers Book 2 | Why Is the Christian Worldview Collapsing in America? | Day 92 | Introduction Worksheet 1 | Name |

Questions

1. Describe how thinking about morality has shifted since America's founding.

2. How can the culture war be fought using Scripture?

3. You are midway through this apologetics course. What are the three most important things you feel you have learned?

4. Why was William Tyndale persecuted, imprisoned, strangled, and his body burned at the stake?

5. Read 1 Chronicles 12:32 — what does it mean to have an understanding of the times? When you think of Christianity in our world or country today, what are your thoughts on how it has been changed — either for better or for worse?

| *The New Answers Book 2* | What Is a Biblical Worldview? | Day 94 | Chapter 1 Worksheet 1 | Name |

Questions

1. Summarize each of the 7 Cs in your own words.

2. How could you personally use the 7 Cs framework in witnessing to the unsaved?

3. How could you personally use the 7 Cs framework in discipling or teaching other Christians?

4. Which of the 7 Cs would you use to explain the following situations from a biblical perspective?

   a. Layers of sedimentary rock in a stream bed

   b. The birth of a mule

   c. Thistles growing along the roadside

   d. A manger scene outside of a church

   e. An evangelistic crusade at a local arena

   f. A rainbow after a storm

   g. Walking through a shopping center and hearing several different languages being spoken

   h. The beauty of a star-filled sky

   i. A nature program showing lions hunting zebras

   j. A disobedient child

| The New Answers Book 2 | What's the Best "Proof" of Creation? | Day 97 | Chapter 2 Worksheet 1 | Name |

Questions

1. Support or refute the claim, "The facts speak for themselves!"

2. What is a presupposition? Who has presuppositions?

3. Develop an analogy for agreeing to a debate without using the Bible.

4. Pick a topic of interest that is related to scriptural authority or creation/evolution. Write a fictitious dialog between yourself and a skeptic of the issue using the Bible and any other relevant evidence.

5. Why is the issue of creation versus evolution not a case of "their facts versus ours"?

| The New Answers Book 2 | Are Biblical Creationists Divisive? | Day 99 | Chapter 3 Worksheet 1 | Name |

Questions

1. Based on the Bible, how should we determine who is the divisive person in a dispute? What Scriptures support this view?

2. What divisive doctrine(s) entered the Church about two hundred years ago?

3. During a discussion someone claims, "Jesus would not teach us to be divided over religious ideas!" How would you respond?

4. What guidance for dealing with divisive individuals do we find in Titus?

5. How does the biblical explanation of unity differ from what is often heard among those in the evangelical community?

| The New Answers Book 2 | How Old Is the Earth? | Day 102 | Chapter 4 Worksheet 1 | Name |

Questions

1. Write a brief description of how the biblical age of the earth is determined.

2. What is the general range for the age of the earth when the Bible is used for the calculation?

3. Who introduced the idea of long ages into the study of the earth's history?

4. How has the secular view of the age of the earth changed over time compared to the biblical age?

5. Are radiometric dating techniques the only uniformitarian methods that set a limit on the age of the earth? How do the ages determined from the other methods compare to the 4.5 billion-year secular age of the earth?

| The New Answers Book 2 | Are There Gaps in the Genesis Genealogies? | Day 104 | Chapter 5 Worksheet 1 | Name |

Questions

1. Why is there a conflict between the genealogies in the Bible and secular history?

2. How has the above conflict impacted the Church?

3. Pick three of the six arguments, and summarize their answers in your own words.

4. How do some creationists try to expand the age of the earth to 10,000 years by using the genealogies?

5. How do the Hebrew words used to indicate relatives in the genealogies get translated into English? What problem does this create?

Questions

1. Identify the objective of the Miller experiment.

2. Explain the oxygen paradox with respect to the naturalistic origin of life.

3. Explain why proteins could not have formed in the primordial oceans.

4. Describe the handedness (chirality) problem encountered in assembling proteins in a naturalistic scenario.

5. Describe the origin of information in all known systems and why this prohibits the origin of life by naturalistic processes.

6. Explain how the laws of probability disprove the naturalistic origin of life hypothesis.

| The New Answers Book 2 | Are Mutations Part of the "Engine" of Evolution? | Day 109 | Chapter 7 Worksheet 1 | Name |

Questions

1. Describe how DNA stores information in the nucleotide sequence of A, C, T, and G.

2. Identify the five basic forms of mutations and the outcome of each in terms of information content. Give an example of each using the sequence ACTGAGCAGTAG.

3. How are proteins, DNA, and amino acids related?

4. Describe key differences between the evolutionary and biblical views on mutations and their role in life.

5. How does the Fall of man connect with the mutations and flaws we see within DNA today?

| The New Answers Book 2 | Did Humans Really Evolve from Apelike Creatures? | Day 113 | Chapter 3 Worksheet 1 | Name |

Questions

1. How do the starting assumptions of evolutionists and Bible-believing Christians influence their understanding of the relationship between apes and humans?

2. Use an analogy to describe the proportion of hominid fossils in the fossil record.

3. Discuss the major differences in anatomy between apes and humans.

4. Research some of the alleged human ancestors that have been exposed as frauds or scientific foibles. Present your information in a chart.

5. Describe the three ways that fossil hominids are treated in order to support human evolution.
   a.

   b.

   c.

| The New Answers Book 2 | Does the Bible Say Anything about Astronomy? | Day 116 | Chapter 9 Worksheet 1 | Name |

Questions

1. Identify instances in the Scriptures that predate recent scientific understanding of the nature of the universe.

2. What do the recession of the moon, magnetic fields, spiral galaxies, and comets show us about the universe?

3. How would you argue for the position that the universe was supernaturally created?

4. Discuss Job 26:7 — read the verse and then share you thoughts on it and pictures of the earth you have seen that were taken from space.

5. Explain the biblical connection to the idea of the universe expanding.

| The New Answers Book 2 | Does the Big Bang Fit with the Bible? | Day 118 | Chapter 10 Worksheet 1 | Name |

Questions

1. Give a brief summary of what happened in the big bang.

2. Identify three inconsistencies that are exposed when people try to fit the big bang into the Bible.

3. In your own words, describe at least three scientific problems with the big bang.

4. Scientific theories are constantly reworked or rejected as new information comes to light. If secular scientists reject the big-bang model in the future, what might be the reaction of a believer who insists that God used the big bang to create the universe?

5. List two additional problems with the big-bang theory.

   a.

   b.

6. You read: "The big bang today relies on a growing number of hypothetical entities, things that we have never observed — inflation, dark matter, and dark energy are the most prominent examples. Without them, there would be a fatal contradiction between the observations made by astronomers and the predictions of the big-bang theory. In no other field of physics would this continual recourse to new hypothetical objects be accepted as a way of bridging the gap between theory and observation. It would, at the least, raise serious questions about the validity of the underlying theory." How has this altered your views on the big bang?

| The New Answers Book 2 | Where Did the Idea of "Millions of Years" Come From? | Day 121 | Chapter 11 Worksheet 1 | Name |

Questions

1. Explain how looking at a road cut could be used to demonstrate the principle of superposition originally described by Niels Steno.

2. Describe the dominant view of the origin of the geologic layers prior to 1800.

3. Distinguish between the catastrophist and the uniformitarian views of geology popular in the 1800s.

4. Describe how most Christians responded to the claims of an old earth.

5. How did the "scriptural geologists" respond to the ideas of an old earth?

6. How would you respond to the statement, "Is there any reason that we can't accept what real geologists have shown to be the true age of the earth?"

| The New Answers Book 2 | What's Wrong with Progressive Creation? | Day 123 | Chapter 12 Worksheet 1 | Name |

Questions

1. List at least four ways that progressive creation is distinct from biblical creation.

    a.

    b.

    c.

    d.

2. Explain how the days of creation in Genesis 1 are twisted by progressive creationists to blend with the big bang.

3. How would you respond to a friend who referred to what we see in nature as the 67th book of the Bible?

4. How does Dr. Ross's use of the words *universal* and *worldwide* mislead people?

5. Why is it necessary for progressive creationists to talk about spiritless hominids? What are they?

6. What passage(s) would you use to show someone that the Flood covered the entire surface of the earth?

| The New Answers Book 2 | Is the Intelligent Design Movement Christian? | Day 126 | Chapter 13 Worksheet 1 | Name |

Questions

1. How does William Paley fit into the discussion of ID?

2. Use the three-step explanatory filter to evaluate:

    a. the human eye

    b. a telephone

    c. paintings found in a cave

3. If an individual is "converted" to believe in intelligent design, which maker/designer would he or she honor?

4. Describe some of the positive and negative aspects of the ID movement from a biblical perspective.

5. Romans 1:20 makes it clear that nature reveals some of the attributes of God as the Creator. Is the knowledge gained by studying nature, and only nature, enough to bring an individual to salvation in Jesus Christ?

6. Review the FAQ section of the Discovery Institute's Center for Science and Culture (http://www.discovery.org/id/faqs/) and read the answer to the question, "Is Discovery Institute a religious organization?" How would you respond to a person who claims that the ID movement is just a cover to promote Christianity?

| The New Answers Book 2 | Can Creationists Be "Real" Scientists? | Day 128 | Chapter 14 Worksheet 1 | Name |

Questions

1. What does the National Academy of Sciences view as the key to understanding biology and the world around us?

2. How does the answer to the question above relate to the real-life experiences and confessions of medical researchers?

3. Discuss the difference between scientific interpretation of historical events and the scientific development of technology and processes.

4. Give some examples of "real" scientists who trust(ed) the Bible to help them understand science. The next time someone claims, "No real scientists believe the Bible is true," you could use these as examples.

5. Which statement do you believe is more accurate? Explain.
    a. Science is only possible because of God.
    b. God can be proven through science.

6. Were you surprised by some of the names on the list of scientists who trusted the Bible? Choose one and research what advances to scientific knowledge he or she is credited with.

| The New Answers Book 2 | How Should a Christian Respond to "Gay Marriage"? | Day 131 | Chapter 15 Worksheet 1 | Name |

Questions

1. What Bible verse gives the answer to the question, "Where did Cain get his wife?" In one sentence, answer the question.

2. What is the fundamental question Christians should ask skeptics when discussing morality?

3. Look up the definition for the philosophy of pragmatism either in a dictionary, or an online dictionary, such as www.merriam-webster.com. What is the source of truth for a pragmatist? Can you identify any areas where you (or others) have based arguments concerning social issues on the results rather than on biblical principles?

4. What danger lies in dealing with social issues from a pragmatic approach?

5. If homosexual marriage is allowed by "majority vote," what other types of relationships might also be allowed in the future?

6. According to the following Bible passages, what is the biblical view of gay marriage?
   a. Genesis 2:18–25
   b. Leviticus 18:22
   c. Mark 10:6
   d. Romans 1:26–27
   e. 1 Corinthians 6:9–10
   f. 1 Timothy 1:9–10

7. How does the study of genetics relate to the gay marriage issue?

8. What is the biblical solution to the gay marriage issue?

| | *The New Answers Book 2* | Did People Like Adam and Noah Really Live Over 900 Years of Age? | Day 134 | Chapter 16 Worksheet 1 | Name |

Questions

1. After which historical event did the longevity of humans begin to decline?

2. Research the biological causes of aging. Prepare a small brochure or chart that communicates the information.

3. What is a genetic bottleneck? What two biblical events have produced this effect?

4. Explain why we might say that "most of the organs in the body of a 90-year-old man are perhaps no older than those of a child."

5. Write a short essay about whether you believe science will ever be able to offer eternal life for humans. Defend your position with biblical and other resources.

| The New Answers Book 2 | Why 66? | Day 137 | Chapter 17 Worksheet 1 | Name |

Questions

1. Why do we refer to the 66 books of the Bible as the canon of Scripture?

2. What evidence supports the exclusion of the Apocrypha as part of the Bible?

3. Why are the Dead Sea Scrolls significant in a discussion of biblical authority?

4. Research the Dead Sea Scrolls to understand how they play an important role in the textual criticism of the Old Testament.

5. What is the difference between the Pentateuch, the Apocrypha, and the Septuagint?

6. How soon was the New Testament recognized, and who named it such?

7. In your own words, describe some of the reasons the canon of Scripture was not formalized quickly.

8. What criteria were used by the early church to decide which books belonged in the canon?

9. What is the ultimate reason behind the Bible being compiled in the way that it has been?

| The New Answers Book 2 | What Was the Christmas Star? | Day 139 | Chapter 18 Worksheet 1 | Name |

Questions

1. Describe some of the physical explanations that have been proposed to explain the star.

2. Does the Christmas star need to be explained by a natural phenomenon? Explain.

3. How is Daniel possibly connected to the magi and the star?

4. Think of the movies or other dramatic presentations of the Christmas account that you have seen in the past. What unbiblical ideas or misconceptions were presented about the star and the magi?

| The New Answers Book 2 | Is Jesus God? | Day 142 | Chapter 19 Worksheet 1 | Name |

Questions

1. How do the names used for God and Jesus in both the Old and New Testaments demonstrate the deity of Jesus?

2. Jesus was worshiped by many while on earth. If Jesus were actually an angel, as claimed by some religions, would He have allowed this worship? Use references from the Bible to support your position.

3. How does the doctrine of the Trinity require that Jesus is God?

4. Pick two of the objections from the chapter and respond to them in your own words.
   a.

   b.

5. List and explain four attributes that Jesus possesses that are those of God.
   a.

   b.

   c.

   d.

| The New Answers Book 2 | Information: Evidence for a Creator? | Day 144 | Chapter 20 Worksheet 1 | Name |

Questions

1. Describe the philosophy of materialism without using any negative words (non-, anti-, reject, not, etc.).

2. Identify each of the following items as material or nonmaterial:

   a. water

   b. logic

   c. light

   d. space

   e. thoughts

   f. emotions

   g. sound

3. How could you demonstrate to someone that information is not part of the material universe?

4. Based on the Universal Definition of Information (UDI), does the Bible contain information? Support your position.

5. Look around the room you are in. Identify two things that clearly meet the UDI standard and two things that are organized, but do not meet the standard.

6. Why is matter necessary to transfer information?

7. How can the existence of information be used to prove evolution false?

| The New Answers Book 2 | Is Evolution a Religion? | Day 147 | Chapter 21 Worksheet 1 | Name |

Questions

1. What is the best evidence for the existence of people who lived in the past?

2. How is observational science related to understanding history?

3. Why are descriptions of the origin of life on earth actually unscientific?

4. Compare the documentation for the evolutionary and biblical explanations of the origin and history of life on earth.

5. Look up the definition of religion, and explain why atheism and evolution fit the definition.

6. Why does evolution appeal to so many as a religious belief?

| The New Answers Book 2 | Is the Bible Enough? | Day 149 | Chapter 22 Worksheet 1 | Name |

Questions

1. How have recent movies, books, and "documentaries" about the Bible worked to undermine the authority of Scripture?

2. What consistency tests does the Apocrypha fail to meet?

3. When *extrabiblical* is used to refer to a book, what is meant?

4. How is gnosticism related to the discussion of extrabiblical writings? What did the Gnostics teach?

5. Cite some examples from gnostic writings that are clearly blasphemous and contrary to Scripture.

6. How do the Mormons and Jehovah's Witnesses view the authority of the Bible?

7. What passages from Scripture would you use to demonstrate the authority of the Word?

| The New Answers Book 2 | Aren't Millions of Years Required for Geological Processes? | Day 152 | Chapter 23 Worksheet 1 | Name |

Questions

1. How does the uniformitarian philosophy view the relationship between the present and the past?

2. What assumption do most people make about the formation of sedimentary rocks? What do observations tell us about their formation?

3. What evidence can be used to support the claim that layered rocks can form rapidly?

4. Research the history of the understanding of the flood that carved the Channeled Scabland region of Washington. How has the view of uniformitarian scientists changed?

5. What conditions are required to form fossils?

6. What is the secular view of the formation of deposits like coal, salts, and reefs?

7. What shift appears to be happening in the community of secular geologists?

| | The New Answers Book 2 | Doesn't Egyptian Chronology Prove That the Bible Is Unreliable? | Day 157 | Chapter 24 Worksheet 1 | Name |

Questions

1. Why is it incorrect to add the length of the reign of the Egyptian pharaohs together to determine the length of the Egyptian dynasties?

2. What types of discrepancies are used to evaluate the authenticity of any history? What should be used as the ultimate standard?

3. What type of flood would have to be described in Genesis if the pyramids are older than the biblical date of the Flood (2348 B.C.)? What other problems are created by the idea of a local flood?

4. By starting from the Bible, what does the revised chronology of Egypt reveal?

5. Why is it important to try to match up the biblical timeline with chronologies like that of Egypt?

6. What was the chronological fact from this chapter you found most interesting, and why?

| The New Answers Book 2 | What about Satan and the Origin of Evil? | Day 159 | Chapter 25 Worksheet 1 | Name |

Questions

1. What other names does the Bible use for Satan?

2. Is it biblical to call Satan an angel?

3. Summarize the biblical argument that identifies when Satan was created. What passages of Scripture are useful in the argument?

4. Is it possible, from a biblical perspective, that Satan fell before the end of day 6 of creation week?

5. According to the Bible, does Satan cause us to sin? Does God cause us to sin?

6. What is the role of Satan after the final judgment?

7. Where will you be after the final judgment? Explain.

| The New Answers Book 2 | Why Is the Scopes Trial Significant? | Day 162 | Chapter 26 Worksheet 1 | Name |

Questions

1. Who were the parties involved in the Scopes trial?

2. What was the essence of the Butler Act?

3. Compare the intentions of Darrow and Bryan for participating in the trials (according to their memoirs).

4. When Bryan was on the stand during the trial, how did Darrow discredit the Bible?

5. What is the significance of this trial for Christians who are interested in apologetics?

| The New Answers Book 2 | Isn't the Bible Full of Contradictions? | Day 164 | Chapter 27 Worksheet 1 | Name |

Questions

1. Explain the "law of noncontradiction" in your own words.

2. What does Psalm 119:160 suggest about the truth of Scripture?

3. Which copies of the Bible would contain no errors?

4. What makes contradictions based on "scientific" reasoning invalid?

5. Why is the context of a verse or phrase important when considering alleged contradictions?

6. Why might it be beneficial to look at many different translations of the Bible to understand an alleged contradiction?

7. What is the result of understanding Scripture (or any text for that matter) if we do not accept that the meanings of words change over time?

8. Is it possible that errors could be introduced into the Bible as it is copied? Does this mean that the Bible contains errors?

| The New Answers Book 2 | Was the Dispersion at Babel a Real Event? | Day 167 | Chapter 28 Worksheet 1 | Name |

Questions

1. How do both Genesis 10:25 and the historian Josephus mentioning Peleg help establish a date for the dispersion of people groups at Babel?

2. What structural evidence found around the world supports the claim that the Tower of Babel was likely a pyramidal structure?

3. How do the names found in the genealogies of different nations around the world compare to the names of the post-Flood generations?

4. What names used around the world today (for regions, people, or languages) reflect names found in the Bible?

5. What is a language family, and how does it relate to the events at Babel?

| The New Answers Book 2 | When Does Life Begin? | Day 169 | Chapter 29 Worksheet 1 | Name |

Questions

1. Identify the three basic positions that describe when life begins.

   a.

   b.

   c.

2. Summarize the basic process of human development in the womb.

3. Why is important to define the terms *fertilization* and *conception* when discussing when life begins?

4. Pick three of the "scientific" views on the beginning of life and explain them in your own words. Why does each of these arguments fail?

Second Semester/Fourth Quarter // 133

5. If science fails in providing a clear answer, what source or authority can we use to answer the question?

6. How does the Bible describe those in the womb?

7. What social/medical issues are related to understanding when life begins?

| The New Answers Book 2 | Do Creationists Believe in "Weird" Physics like ... ? | Day 172 | Chapter 30 Worksheet 1 | Name |

Questions

1. Describe the marks of "good science."

2. Does the scientific method prove things to be true? Explain.

3. How did the "truth" of Newtonian physics change over time?

4. How did Einstein's theories change the understanding of space and time?

5. How does the evidence for string theory compare to the evidence for quantum mechanics and relativity?

| The New Answers Book 2 | Doesn't the Order of Fossils in the Rock Record Favor Long Ages | Day 174 | Chapter 31 Worksheet 1 | Name |

Questions

1. If plants and animals are found fossilized together, what can we solidly conclude?

2. How do evolutionists link asteroids to mass extinctions? What is the biblical perspective on these mass extinctions?

3. How can our current understanding of how life exists in different ecological zones help us to understand the order of life found in the rock record?

4. Based on the biblical description of the Flood, why should we expect to find sea creatures in the lowest fossil-bearing rocks?

5. How does the shape, size, etc., of the creatures being transported determine how the fossil deposits will be organized?

6. What characteristics of vertebrates help to explain their relatively high position in the rock record?

| The New Answers Book 2 | The Biggest Question of All | Day 177 | Conclusion Worksheet 1 | Name |

Questions

1. Compare the need for understanding the issues regarding science and the Bible with a proper understanding of salvation through Christ.

2. Can you remember a point in your life when you repented of your sins before God and put your trust in Jesus Christ to pay for these sins?

   a. If the answer is yes, take a minute to write out a personal testimony and consider sharing it with a friend or relative who is not saved.

   b. If the answer is no, what is keeping you from submitting to God and putting your trust in Christ? Consider talking to a local pastor about the good news of the gospel.

Practical Tests Section

for

Cultural Issues

| The New Answers Book 1 Practical Faith Test | Practical Test 1 | For use after Chapter 6 | Total score: ____ of 100 | Name |

Glossary Exercise: (5 Points Each Question)

The purpose of this activity is to familiarize yourself with the words in the glossary; defending your faith in today's increasingly hostile world means that you have to have more than simple talking points — you have to have an understanding of concepts that enable you to truly defend what you believe.

1. _____ the alleged spontaneous generation of living organisms from non-living matter

2. _____ a physical trait or behavior due to inherited characteristics that gives an organism the ability to survive in a given environment

3. _____ the process of speciation as populations spread and encounter different environments

4. _____ systematic study of the characteristics of humans through history

5. _____ extinct species of perching bird (known from fossils) with teeth, wing claws, and a bony tail

6. _____ an item or its remains produced in the past by humans; generally recovered through archaeological exploration

7. _____ the belief that God, or any supreme intelligence, does not exist

8. _____ genus of extinct apes known from fossils found in Africa, including the infamous "Lucy"

9. _____ a mutation that confers a survival advantage to an organism under certain environmental conditions; usually a result of the loss of genetic information (see mutation)

10. _____ a scientific model based on the biblical account of creation, the curse of nature brought about by Adam's sin, and the global catastrophe of Noah's Flood

11. _____ the cosmological model suggesting the universe began as a single point that expanded to produce the known universe

12. _____ the doctrine that changes in the geologic record are a result of physical processes operating at rates that are dramatically higher than are observed today

13. _____ a theory of biology consisting of three parts: (1) cells are the basic unit of all living things; (2) all living things are composed of one or more cells; and (3) all cells come from preexisting cells

14. _____ reinterpreting Scripture based on outside beliefs and developing theology around this belief. Common origins compromise positions accept the secular view of millions of years, as opposed to the global Flood of Noah. Some of these popular views are: progressive creation/day age theory, gap theory, framework hypothesis, and theistic evolution.

15. _____ the original organisms (and their descendants) created supernaturally by God as described in Genesis 1; these organisms reproduce only their own kind within the limits of preprogrammed information, but with great variation. Note — since the original creation, organisms of one kind cannot interbreed with a different kind, but individuals within a kind may have lost the ability (information) to interbreed due to the effects of the Curse.

16. _____ an extinct people group of Europe and Eastern Asia

17. _____ a belief that all organisms have a single common ancestor that has produced all living organisms through the process of natural selection; popularized by Charles Darwin in *On the Origin of Species*

18. _____ a compromise belief that the days of Genesis 1 are actually vast ages of different lengths; based on secular dating methods

19. _____ a belief in a Creator God that denies His intervention in the history of the universe since its creation

20. _____ an interpretation of Scripture that incorporates the interpreter's ideas as opposed to the actual meaning of the text (taking ideas to Scripture and reinterpreting it)

21. _____ critical interpretation of Scripture taking into account the writing style, meaning, and context of the passage (learning from what Scripture is saying)

22. _____ a type of replacement fossil that includes the concave or convex impression of an organism; typical of shells and leaves

23. _____ an organism in which the porous parts are filled with mineral deposits, leaving the original superstructure intact

24. _____ a compromise belief that Genesis 1 is written in a non-literal, non-chronological way; based on secular dating methods

25. _____ a compromise belief that a vast period of time exists between Genesis 1:1 and 1:2 during which time the geologic eras can be fit

26. _____ the collection of varying alleles within a population of organisms

27. _____ the amount of time required for one-half of the atoms of the parent isotope to decay into the daughter isotope

28. _____ interpreting evidence from past events based on a presupposed philosophical point of view

29. _____ extinct and living members of the family Hominidae, including modern humans and their ancestors

30. _____ fossils of extinct human people groups that are misinterpreted as missing links in human evolution

31. _____ an invalid category consisting of various ape and human fossil fragments

32. _____ the category that includes modern humans, Neandertals, and other extinct human groups

33. _____ a belief in mankind as the measure of all things; based on relative truth and morality and rejecting any supernatural authority

34. _____ the first fossil specimen of *Homo erectus*

35. _____ human remains found in Washington State in 1996

36. _____ anything that contains genetic information, can reproduce offspring that resemble itself, grow and develop, control cellular organization and conditions including metabolism and homeostasis, and respond to its environment. Note — the Bible defines life in a different sense, using the Hebrew phrase *nephesh chayyah*, indicating organisms with a life spirit.

37. _____ term used by evolutionists to describe the alleged, unobservable change of one kind of organism to another by natural selection acting on the accumulation of mutations over vast periods of time

38. _____ term used by evolutionists to describe relatively small changes in genetic variation that can be observed in populations

39. _____ the most recent common ancestor of humans whose lineage can be traced backward through female ancestors; alleged support for the out-of-Africa hypothesis of human evolution

40. _____ the process by which individuals possessing a set of traits that confers a survival advantage in a given environment tend to leave more offspring on average that survive to reproduce in the next generation

41. _____ an extinct human people group with relatively thick bones and a distinct culture; disease and nutritional deficiency may be responsible for the bone characteristics

42. _____ an extension of Darwinism that includes modern genetic concepts to explain the origin of all life on earth from a single common ancestor

43. _____ any compromise position that accepts the millions-of-years idea from secular science and attempts to fit that time into the events of Genesis 1–2

44. _____ a systematic approach to understanding that uses observable, testable, repeatable, and falsifiable experimentation to understand how nature commonly behaves

45. _____ based on the gradual movement of the plates over hundreds of millions of years

46. _____ based on rapid movement of the plates associated with Noah's Flood

47. _____ a compromise belief accepting that God has created organisms in a progressive manner over billions of years to accommodate secular dating methods

48. _____ an evolutionary model that suggests evolution occurs in rapid spurts rather than by gradual change

49. _____ the process of change in a population that produces distinct populations that rarely naturally interbreed due to geographic isolation or other factors

50. _____ the false belief that life can arise from nonliving matter

51. _____ a compromise belief that suggests God used evolutionary processes to create the universe and life on earth over billions of years

52. _____ an explanation of a set of facts based on a broad set of observations that is generally accepted within a group of scientists

53. _____ species that exhibit traits that may be interpreted as intermediate between two kinds of organisms in an evolutionary framework (e.g., an organism with a fish body and amphibian legs)

54. _____ the doctrine that present-day processes acting at similar rates as observed today account for the change evident in the geologic record

55. _____ one of the Hebrew words for "day" encompassing several definitions such as the daylight portion of a day (12 hours, Genesis 1:5a), a day with one evening and one morning (24 hours, Genesis 1:5b), or a longer period of time (Genesis 2:4). The context reveals which definition is in use.

| The New Answers Book 1 Practical Faith Test | Practical Test 2 | For use after Chapter 12 | Total score: ____ of 100 | Name |

Questions: (5 Points Each Question)

1. If you were to try to classify the Bible, what heading you would put it under in a library:
   a) Science
   b) Religious
   c) History
   d) All of the above

2. Why did you make the choice you did — defend the decision, giving four examples or arguments to strengthen your case.
   a)

   b)

   c)

   d)

3. Take a Bible with a concordance or use a concordance online and search for the following words; make note of at least three verses that you find for each:
   a) Stars

   b) Earth

   c) Seas

   d) Moon

   e) Light

   f) Foundation

The goal of the exercise is to become familiar with built-in features of your Bible or other sources of information that can more fully explain important concepts.

4. Find an example of a commentary or footnote that is in your Bible; note the verse selected and then write an explanation of what the commentary or footnote for that verse is telling you, and why it is important information needed in understanding this Scripture.

5. Look up the word *science* in a dictionary or online dictionary that gives the history or etymology of a word. See if you can find out how the word *science* is connected to Genesis 2:9.

| The New Answers Book 1 Practical Faith Test | Practical Test 3 | For use after Chapter 19 | Total score: ____of 100 | Name |

Questions: (5 Points Each Question)

The Historicity of Jesus

Did you know there are some who deny Jesus Christ ever existed? Did you know there are sources other than the Bible that mention Him? Historicity is the fact or historical authenticity of a person or event. Consider the following:

> Christus, from whom the name had its origin, suffered the extreme penalty during the reign of Tiberius at the hands of one of our procurators, Pontius Pilatus, and a most mischievous superstition, thus checked for the moment, again broke out not only in Judæa, the first source of the evil, but even in Rome, where all things hideous and shameful from every part of the world find their centre and become popular. Accordingly, an arrest was first made of all who pleaded guilty; then, upon their information, an immense multitude was convicted, not so much of the crime of firing the city, as of hatred against mankind. Mockery of every sort was added to their deaths. Covered with the skins of beasts, they were torn by dogs and perished, or were nailed to crosses, or were doomed to the flames and burnt, to serve as a nightly illumination, when daylight had expired. Nero offered his gardens for the spectacle, and was exhibiting a show in the circus, while he mingled with the people in the dress of a charioteer or stood aloft on a car. Hence, even for criminals who deserved extreme and exemplary punishment, there arose a feeling of compassion; for it was not, as it seemed, for the public good, but to glut one man's cruelty, that they were being destroyed. (*The Annals* by Roman historian Tacitus)

1. From this passage what do you learn about the historical details of Jesus and at least one Roman emperor's response to Christians? Were the Christians creating violence in the city? How did the punishment of Christians impact non-believers?

2. While you may feel you are attacked or mocked for your beliefs, how is your situation different than that of Christians during Nero's reign?

Now there was about this time Jesus, a wise man, if it be lawful to call him a man; for he was a doer of wonderful works, a teacher of such men as receive the truth with pleasure. He drew over to him both many of the Jews and many of the Gentiles. He was [the] Christ. And when Pilate, at the suggestion of the principal men amongst us, had condemned him to the cross, those that loved him at the first did not forsake him; for he appeared to them alive again the third day as the divine prophets had foretold these and ten thousand other wonderful things concerning him. And the tribe of Christians, so named from him, are not extinct at this day. (*The Antiquities of the Jews*, Book 18, chapter 3 by Flavius Josephus)

3. From reading this excerpt from Josephus, how is it different in tone and description of Jesus than that of Tacitus?

4. How does Josephus' account echo Scripture? In what way does it differ?

. . . this younger Ananus, who, as we have told you already, took the high priesthood, was a bold man in his temper, and very insolent; he was also of the sect of the Sadducees, who are very rigid in judging offenders, above all the rest of the Jews, as we have already observed; when, therefore, Ananus was of this disposition, he thought he had now a proper opportunity [to exercise his authority]. Festus was now dead, and Albinus was but upon the road; so he assembled the sanhedrim of judges, and brought before them the brother of Jesus, who was called Christ, whose name was James, and some others, [or, some of his companions]; and when he had formed an accusation against them as breakers of the law, he delivered them to be stoned: but as for those who seemed the most equitable of the citizens, and such as were the most uneasy at the breach of the laws, they disliked what was done; they also sent to the king [Agrippa], desiring him to send to Ananus that he should act so no more, for that what he had already done was not to be justified; nay, some of them went also to meet Albinus, as he was upon his journey from Alexandria, and informed him that it was not lawful for Ananus to assemble a sanhedrim without his consent. (*The Antiquities of the Jews*, Book 20, chapter 9 by Flavius Josephus)

5. Jesus is mentioned in an indirect way in this passage — how so?

6. Why is it important to know about other sources than the Bible when it comes to talking about the historicity of Jesus?

| The New Answers Book 1 Practical Faith Test | Practical Test 4 | For use after Chapter 25 | Total score: ____ of 100 | Name |

Questions: (5 Points Each Question)

Who Is the Designer?

Basically, intelligent design is a concept where people analyze and look at the forces and aspects of the world and universe, and from the order and integration seen, they can suggest there is an unknown designer. Some think that biblical creation and the intelligent design movement are one and the same, though they are not.

Why is understanding more about this concept important? The following questions will help you work through this analysis:

1. Why isn't recognizing that there is "design" enough?

2. Why is the "designer" not identified?

3. Why do some say this is just another form of creation?

4. Why is acknowledging design in nature not enough when defending your faith in God?

| The New Answers Book 2 Practical Faith Test | Practical Test 5 | For use after Chapter 7 | Total score: ____ of 100 | Name |

Questions: (5 Points Each Question)

Know Your Audience — the Greeks and the Jews

The Bible shows us two different approaches to sharing the gospel through Paul to the Greeks and the Jews. This is important because you need to know who your audience is or the background of the person you are witnessing to in order to be most effective.

The Jewish people had a history of believing in one God who had created everything. So Paul's approach to them was to focus on Jesus being the Messiah. The Greeks, on the other hand, worshiped a number of gods and were focused on philosophies and the form of natural evolution. So for them he needed to lay a foundation of God being the true Creator God, the Fall of man, sin, and the need for a Savior (all of which the Jews were already aware of).

The following exercise is to help you be a more effective witness for Christ. You will be sharing your own testimony and speaking of Christ and the need for a Savior to two audiences. Write a testimony for each, keeping in mind the approaches used to reach the Greeks and the Jews, or do these in an oral form before your family.

1. A group of new friends at a secular summer camp:

2. A church youth group in your hometown:

| The New Answers Book 2 Practical Faith Test | Practical Test 6 | For use after Chapter 15 | Total score: ____ of 100 | Name |

Questions: (5 Points Each Question)

Some Traditional Elements of a Sinner's Prayer

You may one day be in a position to lead someone to Christ by helping him or her say a sinner's prayer. While just saying the sinner's prayer is not what saved you or anyone else, it is the change in our hearts reflected by the prayer that is a first public declaration of faith and acceptance of Christ. There are as many unique sinners' prayers as there are Christians, but many share some common elements. The point of this exercise is to help you think through sample elements and why they are meaningful in terms of faith. Explain why you think the following elements are important:

1. The need for a Savior — the realization we are lost in sin

2. Admitting we have committed sins in our life and need salvation, repenting of our sins

3. Realizing that God is the only one who can offer us forgiveness and grace through Jesus' death on the Cross

4. A willing submission of your life to God — choosing to let God be sovereign in all aspects of your life

5. Receiving the gift of salvation

6. Think about these elements for a few moments, and then compose a sinner's prayer:

| The New Answers Book 2 — Practical Faith Test | Practical Test 7 | For use after Chapter 23 | Total score: ____ of 100 | Name

Questions: (5 Points Each Question)

In the News

Look in the newspaper, on television, or at online news sources to find four different examples of cultural clashes between Christian beliefs and social issues. These can be related to freedom of religion by students in school, or Christian businesses, or even core Christian beliefs at odds with secular ideas and agendas. They do not have to always be negative in nature — for examples, profiles of homeschoolers who have made the choice for religious reasons would be an example of a positive story.

Note the source of the news and the date, and also give a brief summary of what you read or what stood out to you in the news accounts.

1. Source: _____ Date: _____

2. Source: _____ Date: _____

3. Source: _____ Date: _____

4. Source: _____ Date: _____

Conclusion:

1. Were you surprised at the amount or types of cultural stories related to religious liberty or creation that you found? Why or why not?

2. What does your research tell you about the need to be able to defend your faith in effective ways?

| The New Answers Book 2 Practical Faith Test | Practical Test 8 | For use after Chapter 31 | Total score: ____of 100 | Name |

Questions: (5 Points Each Question)

Dinosaurs, an Ark, and the Flood

Some of the most popular questions related to the Bible and its veracity have to do with the accounts of Noah's ark and the Great Flood. Some of the most persistent criticisms of the Bible also center around the Bible and it not mentioning dinosaurs. Refer to the book if needed — or you can search for more information at the Answers in Genesis website, which features a lot of informative articles related to these topics.

1. Why aren't dinosaurs mentioned in the Bible?

2. How could all the animals fit on the ark? (Hint: kinds and size)

3. Is there evidence a global flood even happened?

4. Is there evidence that has been documented that the processes thought to be at work during the Flood can even happen?

5. Did you know that many scientists now feel that a global flood happened on Mars but not on Earth? Why do you think so many are resistant to the idea — because it would mean the Bible is true, or that this would mean their science was faulty?

Essay questions — write a short paragraph answering each question:

Do you think that many reject the concept of a Creator God because that means they would be accountable to Him? If so, why?

Many people start to lose faith in the Bible because they have questions they feel the Bible cannot answer. Can you give three examples of popular doubts about the Bible and how the Bible does give answers for each? (You can use your book and the Internet as needed to gather your answers.)

Semester Tests Section

for

Cultural Issues

| | *The New Answers Book 1*
Practical Faith Test | Semester Test 1 | Scope: Book 1 | Total score: ____ of 100 | Name |

Questions: (5 Points Each Question)

The following questions are taken from the worksheets you completed from *The New Answers Book 1*.

1. Why is a belief in God actually foundational to logical thought and scientific inquiry?

2. The real issue behind saying that God used millions of years of evolution as His method of creation is that it puts the authority of God's Word against man's fallible opinion. How is this true?

3. How is the gap theory different from and similar to the ideas of "theistic evolution" and "progressive creation"?

4. What are some of the common objections to the concept of Cain's wife being a descendant of Adam?

5. How was Noah able to build such a large, seaworthy vessel?

6. Discuss the geological evidences that support a global Flood of Noah's day.

7. Why is it important that we are able to explain the existence of dinosaurs within a biblical worldview?

8. How have evolutionary-based ideas provided support for racism?

9. What is the definition of *natural selection* from an evolutionist's perspective? From a creationist's perspective?

10. How does having an evolutionary foundation impact one's views on death and suffering? How does it impact man's hope for the future?

| *The New Answers Book 2* Practical Faith Test | Semester Test 2 | Scope: Book 2 | Total score: ____ of 100 | Name |

Questions: (5 Points Each Question)

The following questions are taken from the worksheets you completed from *The New Answers Book 2*.

1. How can the culture war be fought using Scripture?

2. What is a presupposition? Who has presuppositions?

3. Write a brief description of how the biblical age of the earth is determined.

4. How does the Fall of man connect with the mutations and flaws we see within DNA today?

5. How do the starting assumptions of evolutionists and Bible-believing Christians influence their understanding of the relationship between apes and humans?

6. Identify three inconsistencies that are exposed when people try to fit the big bang into the Bible.

7. Distinguish between the catastrophist and the uniformitarian views of geology popular in the 1800s.

8. Which statement do you believe is more accurate? Explain.
    a. Science is only possible because of God.
    b. God can be proven through science.

9. Why does evolution appeal to so many as a religious belief?

10. According to the Bible, does Satan cause us to sin? Does God cause us to sin?

11. Why might it be beneficial to look at many different translations of the Bible to understand an alleged contradiction?

Answer Keys for Cultural Issues

The New Answers Book 1 — Worksheet Answer Keys

Glossary – Worksheet 1

1. Answers will vary but a theory is not the same thing as a fact, though it can include factual information about observations that make up a theory. For example, many scientists are convinced there is life on other planets in the universe – they base this theory on the sheer number of planets where conditions might exist that could harbor life, that would have evolved as they feel life evolved here on Earth, but there is no proof there is life anywhere else in the universe. Another example is the theorized evolution of life on Earth.

2. Wording of the answer will vary, but it needs to note that observational science is observable and testable while historical science is where you try to interpret the past using information from a presupposed point of view.

3. Microevolution is the small genetic variations that can be observed in populations, while macroevolution is based on the unobservable idea that one kind of organism can change into another because of natural selection and the accumulations of mutations over a very long period of time.

4. Any compromise position that accepts the millions-of-years idea from secular science and attempts to fit that time into the events of Genesis 1–2. Progressive creation, and theistic evolution.

5. Define the following words:
   a. **exegesis**: a critical interpretation of Scripture taking into account the writing style, meaning, and context of the passage (learning from what Scripture is saying)
   b. **eisegesis**: an interpretation of Scripture that incorporates the interpreter's ideas as opposed to the actual meaning of the text (taking ideas to Scripture and reinterpreting it)
   c. **biblical creation model**: a scientific model based on the biblical account of creation, the curse of nature brought about by Adam's sin, and the global catastrophe of Noah's Flood
   d. **big bang model**: the cosmological model suggesting the universe began as a single point that expanded to produce the known universe

6. A theory of biology consisting of three parts: (1) cells are the basic unit of all living things; (2) all living things are composed of one or more cells; and (3) all cells come from pre-existing cells; answers will vary – for example, if cells come from pre-existing cells, how can a cell suddenly appear for life to begin? Where did it come from?

7. Reinterpreting Scripture based on outside beliefs and developing theology around this belief. Answers will vary, but might include: common origins compromise positions accept the secular view of millions of years, as opposed to the global Flood of Noah. Some of these popular views are: Progressive Creation/Day-Age Theory, Gap Theory, Framework Hypothesis, and Theistic Evolution

Chapter 1 – Worksheet 1

1. Design is not something that happens by chance. Design shows intelligence, and intelligence requires a source. That source, as explained in the Bible, is God.

2. Natural selection and mutations are means of change; however, both of these processes fall short in explaining design because neither can produce new genetic information. Natural selection and mutations involve a loss of genetic information, not a net gain. For something to change from one species into another, information would have to be produced *de novo* and added to the genome. Neither natural selection nor mutations can produce new information. Information always comes from a greater source of information.

3. Genetic information is so complex with every aspect being in the right place, doing the right thing, and doing it at the right time in the right language and in the right order, that if these things aren't just right, the mechanism won't work. The vast amounts of information stored on the DNA molecule must have originated, ultimately, from a source of infinite intelligence.

That source is the Creator of the universe — God, who is not limited in knowledge or wisdom.

4. Logical reasoning and scientific inquiry are only possible in a world created by a logical and scientific Creator. God is self-consistent; He does not contradict Himself. The world He created would then naturally also follow logical and consistent laws. If the world was the result of mutations and chance, random processes, there is no foundation for logic or scientific laws. The very nature of logic comes from the logical and orderly character of its Creator.

5. Faith is believing in something that cannot be seen or fully explained. Faith in God is logical and defensible. Evidence all over the world points to an all-powerful God. Faith in God is not a blind faith that goes against real science. Believing that information can arise from disorder by chance is blind faith since it contradicts real science.

6. Many people have difficulty in accepting a Creator God because if this Creator God did create all things, then all things, including man, would have to obey the rules He places on them. Believing that man arose by chance alleviates this responsibility and man can rule his own life.

Chapter 2 – Worksheet 1

1. Answers should include six of the nine points discussed on pages 26-30 in *The New Answers Book 1*.

2. The idea of the earth being millions of years old is not a new idea. In the 17th and 18th centuries, scientists began to question the biblical truth that the earth was young. One of the first men to develop the idea that the days in Genesis referred to long ages was Comte de Buffon (1708–1788). One of his ideas was that the earth formed as a result of a comet hitting the sun. (For more information on de Buffon and others who taught the idea of an old earth, see www.answersingenesis.org/creation-scientists/british-scriptural-geologists-in-first-half-of-nineteenth-century/.) Comte de Buffon's ideas led the way for many others to question the Scriptures and place their own ideas above God's written Word. Many other ideas of earth history resulted, including the day-age theory, the gap theory, and the ruin-reconstruction theory.

3. Answers will vary, but specific examples should be noted.

4. Answers will vary.

5. Answers will vary.

Chapter 3 – Worksheet 1

1. If you add millions of years into the clear teaching of Scripture, you are picking and choosing what parts of Scripture you want to believe. If you do this in Genesis, then you open the door to picking and choosing what other doctrines and teachings of Scripture you will accept.

2. Believing in millions of years harms the character of God because it says that death, suffering, sickness, and killing were part of the "very good" world before Adam sinned. This means that the God of the Bible is not the loving God who will save us from sin and death. Ultimately, within a long-age view, death is not the penalty for sin, and the suffering, sickness, and pain we see in our world today result because of God's actions, not because of man's actions (sin).

3. Man's fallible opinion allows for millions of years of earth history, but this opinion is strictly that — opinion. Essential to God's character is holiness. He cannot lie, and He cannot deceive. His Word is clear in its teaching. To say that God used evolution in His creation is adding words and ideas of fallible man to the infallible words of God.

4. Answers will vary.

5. Answers will vary.

Chapter 4 – Worksheet 1

1. Answers will vary but should include aspects of or examples of the text noted in the answers or within the text of the book between pages 39–46.

    a. Law of biogenesis

    This law states simply that life always comes from life. This is what observational science tells us; organisms reproduce other organisms after their own kind. According to Genesis 1, God supernaturally created the first diverse kinds of life on earth and made them to reproduce after their kind. Notice that molecules-to-man evolution violates the law of biogenesis. This law is universal — with no known exceptions.

b. Laws of chemistry

Life as we know it would not be possible if the laws of chemistry were different. God created the laws of chemistry in just the right way so that life would be possible. The laws of chemistry give different properties to the various elements (each made of one type of atom) and compounds (made up of two or more types of atoms that are bonded together) in the universe. The properties of elements and compounds are not arbitrary. Atoms and molecules have their various properties because their electrons are bound by the laws of quantum physics. In other words, chemistry is based on physics. If the laws of quantum physics were just a bit different, atoms might not even be possible. God designed the laws of physics just right, so that the laws of chemistry would come out the way He wanted them to.

c. Laws of planetary motion

As with the laws of chemistry, these laws of planetary motion are not fundamental. Rather, they are the logical derivation of other laws of nature. Kepler's laws could be derived mathematically from certain laws of physics — specifically, the laws of gravity and motion (which Newton himself formulated).

d. Laws of physics

There is a hierarchy in physics: some laws of physics can be derived from other laws of physics. For example, Einstein's famous formula $E=mc^2$ can be derived from the principles and equations of special relativity. Conversely, there are many laws of physics that cannot be derived from other laws of physics; many of these are suspected to be derivative principles, but scientists have not yet deduced their derivation. And some laws of physics may be truly fundamental (not based on other laws); they exist only because God wills them to. In fact, this must be the case for at least one law of physics (and perhaps several) — the most fundamental. (Logically, this is because if the most fundamental law were based on some other law, it would not be the most fundamental law.)

e. Universal constants

There are many physical constants of nature. These are parameters within the laws of physics that set the strengths of the fundamental forces (such as gravity), and the masses of fundamental particles (such as electrons). As with the laws of physics, some constants depend on others, whereas some constants are likely fundamental— God alone has set their value. These constants are essential for life. In many cases, if the fundamental constants had a slightly different value, life would not be possible.

f. The anthropic principle

The laws of physics (along with their associated constants) are fine-tuned in just the right way so that life, particularly human life, is possible. This fact is called the "anthropic principle." God created the fundamental laws of physics in just the right way, and gave the constants just the right values so that the other constants and derivative laws of physics would come out in just the right way, so that chemistry would work in the right way, so that the elements and compounds would have the right properties, so that life would be possible!

g. Laws of mathematics

Notice that the laws of physics are highly mathematical in nature. They would not work if there were not also laws of mathematics. Like the laws of physics, some laws and properties of mathematics can be derived from other mathematical principles. But unlike the laws of physics, the laws of mathematics are abstract; they are not "attached" to any specific part of the universe. It is possible to imagine a universe where the laws of physics are different; but it is difficult to imagine a (consistent) universe where the laws of mathematics are different. The laws of mathematics are an example of a "transcendent truth." They must be true regardless of what kind of universe God created. This may be because God's nature is logical and mathematical. Thus, any universe He chose to create would necessarily be mathematical in nature. The secular naturalist cannot account for the laws of mathematics. Certainly, he would believe in mathematics and would use mathematics; but he is unable to account for the existence of mathematics within a naturalistic framework since mathematics is not a part of the physical universe. Mathematics is the "language of creation."

    h. Laws of logic

All the laws of nature, from physics and chemistry to the law of biogenesis, depend on the laws of logic. Like mathematics, the laws of logic are transcendent truths. One cannot imagine that the laws of logic could be anything different than what they are. The atheist cannot account for the laws of logic, even though he or she must accept that they exist in order to do any rational thinking. But according to the Bible, God is logical. Since we have been made in God's image, we instinctively know the laws of logic. We are able to reason logically (though because of finite minds and sin we don't always think entirely logically).

    i. Uniformity of nature

The laws of nature are uniform. They do not change arbitrarily, and they apply throughout the whole cosmos. The laws of nature apply in the future just as they have applied in the past — this is one of the most basic assumptions in all of science. Without this assumption, science would be impossible. If the laws of nature suddenly and arbitrarily changed tomorrow, then past experimental results would tell us nothing about the future. Why is it that we can depend on the laws of nature to apply consistently throughout time? The secular scientist cannot justify this important assumption. But the Christian can; the Bible gives us the answer. God is Lord over all creation and sustains the universe in a consistent and logical way. God does not change, and so He upholds the universe in a consistent, uniform way throughout time (Jeremiah 33:25).

2. Everything in nature is governed by laws. Nothing can function outside these laws. Such governing laws that work in perfect unison cannot be explained in an atheist's worldview because there is no source for such logic and order. Yet, even the atheist must admit that such laws of nature exist.

Chapter 5 – Worksheet 1

1. A gap of indeterminate time is placed between Genesis 1:1 and 1:2.

2. Millions of years of geologic time are placed between the first two verses in Genesis 1.

3. All allow for millions of years of death, disease, and suffering to take place before Adam sinned. All allow fallible theories of scientists to determine the meaning of Scripture. GT accepts that the six days were normal-length days; PC/TE tries to twist the days into representing long ages. GT opposes evolution, TE accepts evolutionary processes (albeit, God-directed).

4. Answers will vary.

5. They choose to accept human teachings over God's Word.

6. Answers will vary.

7. It puts death, disease, and suffering before the Fall, and thus takes away death as a punishment for sin. Why, then, did Jesus suffer a physical death on our behalf?

8. It is inconsistent with God creating everything in six days; it puts death, disease, and suffering before the Fall; it undermines the foundations of the gospel.

9. It ignores the evidence for a young earth; it fails to accommodate standard uniformitarian geology; it does away with evidence for Noah's Flood.

10. *Asah* means "to do" or "to make" and can also mean "to create." *Bara*, when used with God as its subject, means "to create" in the sense of the production of something that did not exist before. They are sometimes used in synonymous parallelism.

11. Genesis 1:2 begins with the Hebrew *waw* which can mean "and," "now," "but," "then," etc. Wherever *waw* precedes a noun (as in v. 2 *waw* "and" + *erets* "the earth"), it has the meaning of an explanation (called a *waw* disjunctive or *waw explicativum*, i.e., explanatory *waw*). It is not a sequence of events such as "then the earth became" (which would require a *waw* consecutive, where *waw* precedes a verb). It

compares with the old English expression "to wit"; it could be translated by "Now" or even with the use of parentheses as follows: "In the beginning God created the heaven and the earth (the earth was without form and empty . . .)." Moses used the two *waw* constructions very deliberately in Genesis 1. Verse 2 has the only *waw* disjunctive. All 28 other verses beginning with "And" have the *waw* consecutive.

For a more detailed treatment of this point, see www.answersingenesis.org/genesis/gap-theory/closing-the-gap/.

12. See www.answersingenesis.org/creationism/old-earth/can-evolutions-long-ages-be-squeezed-into-genesis/ for additional information. This word normally means "was," not "became." In Hebrew, it's much more natural to make a verb out of a noun or adjective to give the idea that some change occurs in something. So if Genesis 1:2 had used *hayethah* to mean "became," the feeling of the language would have been violated, and it would have sounded artificial.

13. They are claimed by gappists to indicate a judgmental destruction rather than something in the process of being built.

14. The English word "replenish" meant "fill" until the 18th century when it began to mean "refill." The Hebrew word used in Genesis 1:28 also meant to "fill," which was the word used in the King James Version of the Bible when it was published in 1611.

Chapter 6 – Worksheet 1

1. Since the Bible describes *all* human beings as sinners, except the God-Man Jesus, and we are all related (Acts 17:26), the gospel makes sense only on the basis that all humans alive and *all* who have ever lived are descendants of the first man Adam. If this were not so, then the gospel could not be explained or defended.

2. Jesus is called "the last Adam" (1 Corinthians 15:45) because He took the place of the first Adam. He became the new head, and because He was sinless, He was able to pay the penalty for sin (1 Corinthians 15:21–22).

3. Cain's wife was either his sister or another close female relative.

4. The law forbidding marriage between close relatives was not given until the time of Moses (Leviticus 18–20). Offspring of brother-sister relationships have an unacceptably high risk of being deformed.

5. God's Laws, biological deformities, etc.; wording may vary but need to touch on these concepts.

6. The related Bible verses do not say he married his wife in Nod, only that they conceived and gave birth to Enoch.

7. Answers will vary but should include examples from the text or the Bible.

Chapter 7 – Worksheet 1

1. Carbon-14 dating is used to date things that were once living.

2. The rate of decay of ^{14}C is such that half of an amount will convert to ^{14}N in 5,730 years. This is the half-life. So, in two half-lives, or 11,460 years, only one-quarter will be left.

   Thus, if the amount of ^{14}C relative to ^{12}C in a sample is one-quarter of that in living organisms at present, then it has a theoretical age of 11,460 years. Anything over about 50,000 years old should theoretically have no detectable ^{14}C left. That is why radiocarbon dating cannot give ages of millions of years. In fact, if a sample contains ^{14}C, it is good evidence that it is *not* millions of years old.

3. That the ratio of ^{14}C to ^{12}C in the atmosphere has always been the same as it is today.

4. Every substance dated by ^{14}C dating would be inaccurately calculated to be older than it really was.

5. The Genesis Flood would have buried large amounts of carbon from living organisms, thus diluting the ratio of ^{14}C to ^{12}C in the atmosphere. The ratio therefore would not have always been constant as assumed.

6. They took samples from ten different coal layers, which evolutionists had dated to be from different time periods in the geologic column. The RATE group tested these samples and found significant amounts of ^{14}C. They also analyzed 12 diamond samples for their ^{14}C content. In both tests, the RATE group concluded that

the samples of coal and diamonds could not be hundreds of millions of years old as claimed.

7. It demonstrates that the earth cannot be many billions of years old.

Chapter 8 – Worksheet 1

1. Because of the claim that the earth is millions/billions of years old.

2. The physical world is suffering from the curse of sin, and therefore is not an accurate portrayal of things as they really were in the beginning. Nature isn't inerrant like the Bible is. See the "General and Special Revelation" section of www.answersingenesis.org/astronomy/the-dubious-apologetics-of-hugh-ross/.

3. Because it elevates the ideas and assumptions of sinful men to a position above the inerrant Word of God. We must allow Scripture to speak to us, rather than making Scripture say what we want it to say. See www.answersingenesis.org/the-word-of-god/nature-67th-book-of-bible/.

4. *yom; Qedem, olam, dor, tamid, ad, orek, shanah, netsach*

5. *yom*

6. A word can have many meanings depending on the context in which it is used. Context helps determine the meaning.

7. Answers will vary.

8. See chart on page 110 of text book.

9. Theistic evolution is the idea that God used evolutionary processes over millions of years to form the world and its inhabitants. It denigrates the character/nature of God, denies the authority of the Bible, destroys the basis of the gospel message, makes God a "god of the gaps," does away with biblical chronology, contradicts and opposes God's omnipotent acts of creation, misrepresents reality, misses the purpose of man, and the biblical order is different from evolutionary order of creation events. See www.answersingenesis.org/creationism/old-earth/ for additional information.

10. PC is the idea that the days of Genesis 1 represent creation periods in which God progressively created the world and its inhabitants over millions of years. The order of events in Genesis differs from the order of events as related by "science." It destroys the basis of the gospel, denies scriptural authority, damages the character/nature of God, etc.

11. This view gives Scripture its proper authority and allows us to accept and make sense of the rest of God's Word.

Chapter 9 – Worksheet 1

1. Measurements of the amounts of parent and daughter elements are taken and an age is assigned based on certain assumptions.

2. Igneous rocks; see www.answersingenesis.org/geology/radiometric-dating/radio-dating-in-rubble/ for additional information.

3. The time it takes for half of the amount of the parent element to decay into the daughter element.

4. 1) The initial conditions of the rock samples are accurately known; 2) the amount of parent or daughter elements in a sample has not been altered by processes other than radioactive decay; and 3) the radioactive decay rate of the parent isotope has remained constant since the rock was formed. See www.answersingenesis.org/geology/carbon-14/radioactive-dating-failure/ for additional information.

5. You would reach incorrect dates.

6. This form of dating involves analyzing four or more samples from the same rock unit in order to eliminate the assumption of starting conditions by using ratios and graphs.

7. The RATE group conducted experiments to find the amount of helium in granite rocks. The zircon crystals in granite rocks contain radioactive uranium which decays into lead. As it decays, the uranium, releases helium atoms. Because the decay of uranium into lead is such a slow process, at today's rates little or no helium should have remained in the granite. But when tested, RATE scientists found significant amounts of helium.

Chapter 10 – Worksheet 1

1. The intelligence and physical strength of the people of Noah's day were likely at least equal to, if not superior to, ours today. There is no reason

why Noah and his sons couldn't have built the ark on their own. They also could have hired skilled laborers to help build the ark. Also, keep in mind that these people were not primitive in any way. Their tools, machines, and building techniques were completely sufficient and effective to build such a huge vessel.

2. On the ark: land animals, creeping things (reptiles), and flying creatures; not on the ark: sea creatures, insects, other invertebrates, and plants.

3. From Genesis 1, the ability to produce offspring (i.e., to breed with one another) defines the original created kinds. If two animals or two plants can hybridize (at least enough to produce a truly fertilized egg), then they must belong to (i.e., have descended from) the same original created kind. If the hybridizing species are from different genera in a family, it suggests that the whole family might have come from the one created kind. If the genera are in different families within an order, it suggests that maybe the whole order may have derived from the original created kind. Creationists estimate that the number of animals on the ark ranged from a few thousand to 35,000.

4. There was plenty of space for the animals, and animals that we consider to be primarily meat eaters could have eaten plant materials of some kind or dried meat, while others could have eaten hay, seeds, or vegetables of some kind. With plenty of room, Noah could have taken plenty of food supplies for the animals in his care. Any number of innovations could have been built into the ark to make feeding and watering the animals easier and more efficient in terms of time and labor. See https://answersingenesis.org/noahs-ark/caring-for-the-animals-on-the-ark/.

5. When reading the biblical account of Noah, have you ever wondered why God gave some specific details on how large the ark should be and other aspects of its design? Tests have shown it would have been very seaworthy. See www.answersingenesis.org/noahs-ark/safety-investigation-of-noahs-ark-in-a-seaway/.

6. The water came from "the fountains of the deep" and from "the windows of heaven."

7. Genesis 7:19–20; Matthew 24:37–39; 2 Peter 3.

8. The earth's terrain, from canyons and craters to coal beds and caverns, indicates a catastrophic history. Layers of strata show that they were laid down by water, and fossils buried in these layers give evidence to an extremely rapid burial.

Chapter 11 – Worksheet 1

1. The animals came to the ark (Genesis 6:20). It was divinely controlled.

2. Fossilization of animal remains is not a given rule. For animal remains to be fossilized, they must be buried quickly in sediment, or the bones would decompose before they were permineralized.

3. As animals moved out from the mountains of Ararat, they would have most likely travelled by land. As the Ice Age set in, land bridges likely connected separate landmasses, giving animals a means to get to different continents.

4. The Recolonization Theory claims that none of the present fossils were caused by the Flood since the Flood completely obliterated the earth's crust. The theory then says that the fossil record is a record of processes that happened after the Flood when the earth was being recolonized. The error of this theory is its faulty starting point. It starts with the fossil record instead of with Scripture. This theory can easily lead to compromises, one of which has been that there are gaps in the genealogies in Genesis 5 and 11. For more information about the Recolonization Theory, see www.answersingenesis.org/bible-timeline/genealogy/the-recolonisation-theory-the-latest-compromise/.

5. Answers will vary.

Chapter 12 – Worksheet 1

1. Answers will vary.

2. Origins: speculating about dinosaurs evolving into birds, figuring out how long ago dinosaurs lived; operational: excavating bones, finding places of burial.

3. It refers to "dragons" and a creature called "behemoth" (Job 40), which some believe refers to dinosaurs.

4. A number of examples have been found of dinosaur bones that still have soft tissue, cells, or connective tissue that have been well preserved and defy an explanation of being fossilized for tens of millions of years. See www.answersingenesis.org/dinosaurs/bones/ostrich-osaurus-discovery/.

5. If we accept God's Word, beginning with Genesis as being true and authoritative, then we can explain dinosaurs and make sense of the evidence we observe in the world around us. In doing this, we are helping people see that Genesis is absolutely trustworthy and logically defensible, and is what it claims to be — the true account of the history of the universe and mankind. And what one believes concerning the Book of Genesis will ultimately determine what one believes about the rest of the Bible. This, in turn, will affect how a person views him or herself, and fellow human beings, and what life is all about, including his or her need for salvation.

Chapter 13 – Worksheet 1

1. Factors include the fact that the majority of fossils in the fossil record are marine organisms, the truth that human fossilization is rare since humans are mobile creatures and would have been unlikely to be buried rapidly by water, and the fact that humans probably did not inhabit the areas where dinosaurs lived. These factors are significant because they would change the likelihood for human fossils and dinosaur fossils to be found together.

2. No, such a claim neglects the other factors involved.

3. Post-Flood.

4. Relatively small compared to other fossils found.

5. *māhâ*

6. A small human population and massive amounts of sediment are two prominent factors why we haven't found human fossils in pre-Flood sediments.

7. No. In the old-earth view, man isn't supposed to be the same age as dinosaurs. Yet we can be sure that this finding would not overturn their starting assumptions — they would simply try to develop a hypothesis consistent with their preconceived view of history. For example, they might search for the possibility that the fossils were moved and redeposited.

So, ultimately, the debate is not about the evidence itself — where we find human fossils and dinosaur fossils. Nobody was there to actually observe humans and dinosaurs living together outside of written revelation, which is very limited pre-Flood.

Chapter 14 – Worksheet 1

1. Answers will vary.

2. Extension: rifting or moving apart; transform faulting: horizontal slippage along a large fault line; subduction: one plate plunging beneath another. Extension is caused by the seafloor being pulled apart. Transform faulting is caused by one plate sliding horizontally past another. Compression is caused by two plates moving toward one another.

3. Antonio Snider first suggested the idea of continental drift in the 1800s, but it went relatively unnoticed. Alfred Wegener further supported this theory in the early 1900s. But it wasn't until the mid-1960s that experiments and measurements were done that brought about the birth of the theory of plate tectonics.

4. Zebra-striped magnetic patterns in the seafloor could not have been the result of slow and gradual plate tectonics. The floors of trenches are not compressed, deformed, or thrust-faulted; they are instead soft, flat-lying sediments, which is consistent with rapid plate tectonics. For more information, see www.answersingenesis.org/geology/plate-tectonics/.

5. The Bible does not directly mention catastrophic plate tectonics; however, in Genesis 1:9–10 it does suggest that the continents were at one time one supercontinent. This suggestion leads to the only possibility of rapid continental division during the Flood. Genesis 10:25 mentions that "the earth was divided," but the context of this passage of Scripture deals with the dividing of the people groups at the Tower of Babel, not the dividing of the continents. Catastrophic plate tectonics is consistent with the Bible.

Chapter 15 – Worksheet 1

1. Answers will vary.
2. Isaiah 40:22 and Job 26:10
3. The humanists later revived this strange belief during the Renaissance and tried to imply that Christians, for the most part, believed this view. However, this simply wasn't the case. Instead, the humanists took some biblical passages out of context.
4. A mutation that causes a beetle to lose its wings would be considered beneficial if the beetle lived on a windy island. It would be beneficial because it might keep the beetle from blowing out to sea to die. However, this mutation causes a loss of genetic information since the beetle no longer has the information to make wings. It could also be considered a harmful mutation since it can't get away from predators as easily. The mutation that causes sickle cell anaemia could be considered beneficial because it protects against malaria. However, the person with this mutation has lost the information to make proper, efficient blood cells, and sickled blood cells cause many problems.
5. No. It does not.
6. If you give up this foundation of starting with the Bible and you insert evolutionary/millions-of-years ideas for the past history of the world over the Bible's teachings in Genesis, it is inconsistent to believe the rest of the Bible — particularly the gospel.

Chapter 16 – Worksheet 1

1. To develop an ice age, where ice accumulates on the land, the oceans need to be warm at mid- and high-latitude, and the landmasses need to be cold, especially in the summer. Warm oceans evaporate lots of water, which then moves over the land. Cold continents result in the water precipitating as snow rather than rain, and also prevent the snow from thawing during summer. The ice thus accumulates quickly.

   We would expect warm oceans at the end of the global Flood, due to the addition of hot subterranean water to the pre-Flood ocean and heat energy released through volcanic activity. Large amounts of volcanic dust and aerosols from residual volcanic eruptions at the end of and after the Flood would have reflected solar radiation back into space, causing low temperatures over land, and especially causing the summers to be cold. Dust and aerosols slowly settle out of the atmosphere, but continued post-Flood volcanism would have replenished these for hundreds of years following the Flood.

   Vardiman has shown, using standard knowledge of atmospheric circulation, that the warm oceans after the Flood, and the large rates of cooling at the poles, would have driven extreme atmospheric convection. This would have created an enormous polar hurricane-like storm system covering a large portion of the Arctic. This, he suggests, could have functioned for much of the 500-year period up to the glacial maximum. Such circulation patterns would have delivered to the higher latitudes the vast amounts of snow that would have quickly become ice sheets, spreading firstly over the continents, and then later over the oceans as the water cooled toward the end of the glacial period.

2. Evidences are lateral moraines, terminal moraines, and scratched bedrock and boulders.
3. According to most secular/uniformitarian scientists, there were 30 or more ice ages over the past few million years, with periods of warmth between. Most secular glaciologists believe that there were eight ice ages over the past 800,000 years, and each lasted 100,000 years. They also believe that there were four ancient ice ages that occurred hundreds of millions to several billion years ago, with each ice age lasting tens to hundreds of millions of years.
4. The effects of *the* Ice Age are still with us, particularly the giant ice sheets of Antarctica and Greenland, the alpine glaciers, and the glacial landforms and sediments. Because these effects are seen on the current land surface, it is clear that the Ice Age occurred after the Flood.
5. It lasted approximately 700 years.
6. Job 37:9–10, 38:22–23, 29–30
7. The post-Flood Ice Age provides an explanation for the mystery of the woolly mammoths, as well as many other Ice Age mysteries. The mammoths spread into these northern areas

during early and middle Ice Age time because summers were cooler and winters warmer. The areas were unglaciated (just the mountains glaciated) and a rich grassland. However, late in the Ice Age, winter temperatures turned colder and the climate drier with strong wind storms. The mammoths died by the millions and were buried by dust, which later froze, preserving the mammoths. See www.answersingenesis.org/extinct-animals/ice-age/.

8. When Lake Missoula, which had formed as a result of the Ice Age, burst and emptied in a few days, the rushing waters rapidly carved out canyons and produced many flood features on the earth's surface. The impact of this local flood on its surrounding area gives us a small-scale glimpse of the impact the global Flood had on the earth's entire surface.

Chapter 17 – Worksheet 1

1. One of the biggest justifications for racial discrimination in modern times is the belief that people groups have evolved separately. Thus, different groups are at allegedly different stages of evolution, and so some people groups are more backward than others. Therefore, the other person may not be as fully human as you.

2. Answers will vary.

3. God instituted marriage because it was not good for man to be alone; so He created a helper for the first man, Adam. One purpose of marriage is to produce godly offspring.

4. Canaan received the curse. Noah may have seen some of the same sin problems in Canaan as he did in Ham. No, black people are not the result of the curse on Ham.

5. Rahab was a Canaanite. These Canaanites had an ungodly culture, and were descendants of Canaan, the son of Ham. Remember, Canaan was cursed because of his obvious rebellious nature. Sadly, many Christians state that Ham was cursed — but this is not true. Some have even said that this (non-existent) curse of Ham resulted in the black "races." This is absurd and is the type of false teaching that has reinforced and justified prejudices against people with dark skin.

In the genealogy in Matthew 1, it is traditionally understood that the same Rahab is listed here as being in the line leading to Christ. Thus, Rahab, a descendant of Ham, must have married an Israelite (descended from Shem). Since this was clearly a union approved by God, it underlines the fact that the particular people group she came from was irrelevant — what mattered was that she trusted in the true God of the Israelites.

The same can be said of Ruth, who as a Moabitess, also married an Israelite, and is also listed in the genealogy in Matthew 1 that leads to Christ. Prior to her marriage, she had expressed faith in the true God (Ruth 1:16). When Rahab and Ruth became children of God, there was no longer any barrier to Israelites marrying them, even though they were from different people groups.

6. If one wants to use the term *interracial*, then the real interracial marriage that God says we should not enter into is when a child of the Last Adam (one who is a new creation in Christ — a Christian) marries one who is an unconverted child of the First Adam (one who is dead in trespasses and sin — a non-Christian).

Chapter 18 – Worksheet 1

1. With an evolutionary mind-set, the earth is simply another planet in the vast universe. It just happened to have the right conditions for life to evolve. This would open the possibility for life to evolve on other planets in the universe. But God created the earth to sustain life; no other planet is like it.

2. If life exists on other planets, how would these extraterrestrials be saved? If they are not descendants of Adam, they are not blood relatives of Jesus, and therefore Jesus' blood cannot pay for their sin. However, they are affected by Adam's sin because the Bible is clear that all creation is under the effects of the Curse. If one believes in alien life, these beings are without hope of salvation.

3. Finding extraterrestrial life would prove evolution, from an evolutionist's perspective.

4. In Genesis 1 we read that God created plants on the earth on day 3, birds to fly in the atmosphere and marine life to swim in the ocean on day

5, and animals to inhabit the land on day 6. Human beings were also made on day 6 and were given dominion over the animals. But where does the Bible discuss the creation of life on the "lights in the expanse of the heavens"? There is no such description because the lights in the expanse were not designed to accommodate life. God gave care of the earth to man, but the heavens are the Lord's (Psalm 115:16).

5. Since there are quite possibly multiple billions of planets in our galaxy, and since in the secular view these are all accidents, it is almost inevitable that some of these had the right conditions for life to evolve. And if some of these worlds are billions of years older than ours, then at least some of them would have evolved intelligent life eons ago. The universe should therefore have countless numbers of technologically superior civilizations, any one of which could have colonized our galaxy ages ago. Yet we find no evidence of these civilizations. Where is everybody? This problem has become known as the "Fermi paradox."

Chapter 19 – Worksheet 1

1. It would mean that whenever we look at the behavior of a very distant object, what we see happening never happened at all. This would mean that for a 10,000-year-old universe, anything we see happening beyond about 10,000 light-years away is actually part of a gigantic picture show of things that have not actually happened, showing us objects that may not even exist. It is like saying that God created fossils in rocks to fool us, or even test our faith, and that they don't represent anything real (a real animal or plant that lived and died in the past). This would be a strange deception.

2. a. The speed of light is and always has been constant. If the speed of light changes, the ratio of energy to mass also changes. It may also have other implications that are not fully known.

   b. Time flows at the same rate in all conditions. This is a false assumption because when an object moves very fast, close to the speed of light, its time is slowed down (time dilation). Therefore, light measured to take billions years to reach earth, as measured by clocks in deep space, could reach earth in only thousands of years as measured by clocks on earth.

   c. All time is synchronized. There is no method by which two clocks that are separated by distance can be synchronized in an absolute sense. This would change the results of "measured" time.

   d. All that is can be explained by natural processes. However, this assumption overlooks the power of the Creator God. It says that everything can be explained by natural laws and processes, but God worked outside those boundaries during creation week.

3. There are two measurements of time. Universal time is how time affects all places on the earth at the same time. Local time is how a certain region measures time. For example, a plane leaving one location at 4:00 p.m. local time can spend two hours (universal time) in the air before landing at another location at 4:00 p.m. local time. With light traveling toward earth, it always remains at the same local time, but it is always gaining in universal time.

4. God created the world to follow natural laws because He is a God of order and design. Since He created those natural laws, He is not bound by them; He is above them.

5. In the big-bang model, light must travel a much greater distance than should be possible within the big bang's own time frame.

6. This is the idea that there are two expansion rates to allow for two points at great distances in the universe to be the same temperature. No, this idea has no supporting evidence, and it only adds to the problems and difficulties of the big-bang model.

7. No.

Chapter 20 – Worksheet 1

1. Mark 10:6, 13:19; Luke 4:25–27, 11:50–51, 13:14, 17:28–32; John 3:14, 5:45–47, 6:32–33, 49; Matthew 10:15, 12:40–41, 19:3–6, 24:38–39; Exodus 20:11.

2. Adam and Eve as the first married couple; Abel as the first prophet who was killed; Noah and the Flood; Moses and the serpent in the wilderness; Moses and the manna from heaven to feed the Israelites; the experiences of Lot and his wife; the

judgment of Sodom and Gomorrah; the miracles of Elijah; and Jonah and the big fish. Jesus claiming these events as historical fact give these accounts validity in the New Testament, and Jesus used them to teach His disciples that real events, like His death, Resurrection, and Second Coming, would also come to pass.

3. The Jewish people at the time believed that the first day of creation and the creation of Adam were about 5,000 years before Christ. We know this from the writings of Josephus. (See footnote 1 on page 255 of *The New Answers Book* Vol. 1.)

4. Answers will vary.

5. Answers will vary.

Chapter 21 – Worksheet 1

1. If defense/attack structures are the results of God's design, God is the author of bloodshed, death, and pain. How could a good God be the author of such things?

2. No, sin changed the world.

3. Genesis 3:14 — The serpent was cursed *more* than other animals; all the other animals were cursed, too. Genesis 3:16 — Pain and sorrow in childbearing and raising children was increased. Genesis 3:17–19 — The ground is cursed. Death begins.

4. Defense/attack structures could have been used for other purposes before the Fall. They also could have been brought in by God as a result of the Fall.

5. God promised a way of redemption. In Genesis 3:15, He promised a Savior to be born of a woman.

Chapter 22 – Worksheet 1

1. Natural selection, according to evolutionists, is defined as evolutionary change or the driving force behind evolutionary change. According to creationists, natural selection is the process whereby organisms with certain characteristics survive better in a given environment or under a given selective pressure.

2. Edward Blyth, a creationist, described natural selection from a biblical perspective. Blyth believed and wrote that natural selection did not create new information or a new organism but that it was a means of conserving an already created organism.

3. The genetic diversity within the created animal kinds gave these animals the best chance of surviving in a world that was greatly altered by the Flood and its after-effects.

4. Changing from one organism into a completely different organism, as required by evolution, requires natural selection to create new information. However, natural selection cannot fulfill this requirement. Natural selection is limited in what it can do, as is expected in the biblical creation model.

5. A species is a population of organisms produced by a parent population that has changed so significantly that it can no longer interbreed with the parent population.

6. New species can form in just a few years. Such an observation supports a young earth because all the species in the past and today must have come from the original created kinds only 6,000 years ago.

Chapter 23 – Worksheet 1

1. The biblical account of creation is at total odds with the evolutionary time scale. One is correct, and the other is wrong.

2. The big bang claims that life can arise from nothing, but life being formed within a vacuum does not support this claim because a vacuum is something.

3. Miller's experiment made assumptions about the conditions of the atmosphere — certain gases were present and oxygen was completely absent. Also, he failed to form only left-handed amino acids, which are what make up living organisms.

4. It is the science that deals with the structure of animals. Differences in structure show that structures were designed to fulfill different purposes. Animals with similar structures are evidence that they have the same Designer, not that they are related to one another.

5. Darwin's findings support the Bible-based teaching that finches reproduce after their own kind. They did not support his ideas of molecules-to-man evolution.

Chapter 24 – Worksheet 1

1. From carefully reading the Bible, we learn that different dinosaur kinds were created on day 6 along with the other land animal kinds, while the different bird kinds were created on day 5. Evolutionists claim that birds evolved from dinosaurs.

2. Dinosaurs are cold-blooded, but birds are warm-blooded creatures that maintain a relatively constant internal temperature. The temperature of a bird's blood is also exceptionally high compared to other warm-blooded creatures. However, dinosaurs, along with other reptiles, have a varying body temperature based on their surrounding environment. Bird-hipped dinosaurs have pubic bones that are directed toward the rear, but even these dinosaurs are even less bird-like than the lizard-hipped dinosaurs. Birds with three-fingered "hands" have a set of three different fingers than theropod dinosaurs that have three fingers. Dinosaurs had fingers, 1, 2, and 3 while birds have 2, 3, and 4. Birds' lungs are small and rigid, yet they are extremely efficient. Their respiration includes "flow-through ventilation," which moves air into air sacs, which then move the air through the lungs. Dinosaurs' lungs, however, have been shown to be similar to reptiles, not birds.

    Birds' lungs are small and rigid, yet they are extremely efficient. Their respiration includes "flow-through ventilation," which moves air into air sacs, which then move the air through the lungs. Dinosaurs' lungs, however, have been shown to be similar to reptiles, not birds.

3. *Archaeopteryx*. It is a true bird.

4. An ectothermic animal can adjust its body temperature behaviorally (e.g., moving between shade and sun), even achieving higher body temperature than a so-called warm-blooded animal, but this is done by outside factors.

5. There have been claims to that effect but no evidence in the fossil record. Structures called protofeathers have been noted, but they are not feathers. They are now thought to be connective tissue fibers. But if one should be found it would only impact how we classify these animals, but not call into question the veracity of the Bible.

6. Birds, which tells us that God didn't create them from dinosaurs because dinosaurs were not yet created. Genesis is clear that God didn't make birds from pre-existing dinosaurs. In fact, dinosaurs (land animals made on day 6) came *after* winged creatures made on day 5, according to the Bible.

Chapter 25 – Worksheet 1

1. It is written communication from God to man.

2. Answers may vary but should include information related to Enuma Elish, Epic of Gilgamesh, Sumer king's list.

3. Answers may vary but should include information related to excavation of Ur, customs of the times reflected in the archaeological finds at Ur, Mari, Boghazhoi, Nineveh; Sarah approaching Abraham about Hagar bearing him a child; records of the five kings who fought against four kings; negotiations with the Hittites; use of hanakim.

4. Answers may vary but should include information related to known Egyptian titles, other Egyptian recorded ceremonies; Dead Sea Scrolls - Genesis 46:27.

5. Answers may vary but should include information related to Law of Moses, convenant forms of writing like the Hittites, experiences of Professor Nelson Glueck & Professor George Ernest Wright; 10 plagues of Egypt against the leading gods of Egypt.

6. Answers may vary but should include information related to deities such as Baal, Asherah, and Dagan associated with the right people; city-states identified correctly; Saul's head and armor placed in two temples at Beth-Shan and Philistine and Canaanite temples being found there.

7. Answers may vary but should include information related to David's elegy reflected the appropriate literary style as shown by excavations Ras Shamra (Ugarit); correct dating of Psalms because of the discovery of the Ugaritic library; discovery and excavation of Solomonic cities like Hazor, Megiddo, Gezer, and similar blueprints.

8. Answers may vary but should include information related to discovery of Sargon's palace at Khorsabad, wall inscription and library

record for the battle against Ashdod; Assyrian titles as used by biblical writers, many of which were considered "obsolete"; confirmation of Sennacherib in the records of his sons; details of Nineveh; connections with Adad-Nirari and Jonah.

9. Answers may vary but should include information related to Daniel knowing Nebuchadnezzar was responsible for the splendor of Babylon even though it wasn't confirmed by excavations 100; information in the Babylonian Chronicle; prophecies against Babylon have been fulfilled.

10. Answers may vary but should include information related to Cyrus being proven to have existed and his tomb being found; the Cyrus Cylinder; Aramaic documents from Egypt showing some Jews remained in Babylon.

11. Answers may vary but should include information related to Elephantine papyri, the Dead Sea Scrolls, Targums of Job, etc., show that Aramaic was then in use; Sanballat was, as the Bible says, the governor of Samaria (Nehemiah 4 and 6), though it was claimed by many writers that Sanballat was much later than Nehemiah. Several Sanballats are now known, and recovered letters even refer to Johanan and Geshem; proper dating of Artaxerxes I.

12. Answers may vary but should include information related to discovery and analysis of the Dead Sea Scrolls; that they were created 1000 years than other known Hebrew copies, and the use of the language (common uses and older forms); and they detailed many of the Assyrian palaces that were not found until after 1840.

13. Answers may vary but should include information related to documents to the census taken at that time have been uncovered in embalmed crocodiles in Egypt, which were Jewish priestly writings; history provided on the timing of the census, the usage of the language Christ used; Pilate and references to him uncovered at Caesarea — the John Rylands papyrus.

14. Answers may vary but should include information related to the papyri from those Egyptian "talking crocodiles" help confirm usage of the language at the time among everyday people; findings by Sir William Ramsay and his successors in Asia Minor re-established the veracity of Luke the historian and other New Testament writers; Ezra/Nehemiah, and Luke have been remarkably confirmed as being accurate and reliable by the research of credible scholars; lots of evidences of continuity between the New Testament documents, as well as evidence from the writings of secular Roman writers and early church fathers.

15. Answers may vary but should include information related to archaeology confirming Bible history, and it often shows that Bible people and incidents are correctly referred to; archaeology gives local color, indicating that the background is authentic; archaeology provides additional facts; archaeology has proved of tremendous value in Bible translations; archaeology has demonstrated the accuracy of many Bible prophecies.

16. S-Superiority, C-Customs, A-Additional information, L-language and languages, P-Prophecy, and S-Specific incidents and people.

Chapter 26 – Worksheet 1

1. It is defined as: soul, self, life, creature, person, appetite, mind, living being, desire, emotion, passion. It is used in Genesis 1 as; 1) that which breathes, the breathing substance or being, soul, the inner being of man 2) living being 3) living being whose life resides in the blood 4) the man himself (self, person, or individual) 5) seat of the appetites 6) seat of emotions and passions 7) mental acts 8) acts of the will (dubious) 9) character (dubious)*

   * The Brown-Driver-Briggs Hebrew and English Lexicon, Hendrickson Publishers, 1996, pp. 659–661. It is used to convey the basic idea of a breathing creature.

2. Cattle, birds of the air, beasts of the field

3. Because plants aren't "alive" in the biblical sense — they don't possess *nephesh* life.

4. Adam's sin — and ours — is the root cause of the death and suffering in the world today; see www.answersingenesis.org/go/death-suffering for

additional information.

5. Sin impacted the entire earth because it brought with it a curse. Romans 8:22 says that all creation groans in pain, and Romans 5:12 says that death spread to all men — both past and present. Our world continues in this cursed state until God creates a new heaven and a new earth.

6. Since evolution places death before Adam and Eve sinned in the Garden of Eden, death has always existed and impacted the earth and mankind. There is no beginning of it, and there is no ending to it. Man is simply the end result of millions of years of death and suffering. With this belief system as one's foundation, there is no future hope for mankind.

7. The hope for suffering Christians is that the suffering and pain they are enduring will one day end. For now, they can trust in the truth that God loves them and has a purpose for them and that He has something for them to learn through the suffering and pain of their trials.

Chapter 27 – Worksheet 1

1. Someone familiar with the basic teachings of Christianity

2. Someone unfamiliar with the basic teachings of Christianity

3. They believed in the God of creation and the consequences of man's sin. They also knew what was expected of them in the Law and how they fell short of that expectation. They also knew and practiced the religious rite of animal sacrifice to cover their sins.

4. Peter focused his message on Jesus' work on the Cross.

5. The Greeks believed in many gods, and they believed that these gods, along with mankind, evolved. They had no basis for sin or for what could atone for their sin.

6. Paul laid the foundation of Scripture, starting from the beginning. He preached about the true God, Adam's sin, all mankind being related, and man's need for redemption.

7. At one time, modern nations had a basic knowledge of God, man's sin, morality, the need for redemption, etc. However, these same nations now have very little knowledge about the truths of the Bible. Instead, they have accepted their own ideas as ultimate truth.

8. It must address the faulty foundation of the "Greek" culture with God being Creator.

9. Answers will vary.

Bonus Chapter – Worksheet 1

1. Answers will vary, but you need to provide both a biblical foundation for your answer (Scripture or scripturally based truths) — like what day the dinosaurs would have been made per the information we have in the Bible — and how the Bible can be trusted. It is also important to note that the word "dinosaur" did not even exist when the Bible was originally written. It wasn't until 1841 when Sir Richard Owen gave this name to the small group of fossil specimens that had been found by that time. He called them *dinosauria*, which means "terrible lizard". You may also want to include Scripture that includes Job 40:15-20 (behemoth) and Job 41 (leviathan). Or use dinosaurs to discuss the events of the Great Flood and Noah's Ark.

2. Answers will vary, but the Flood of Noah is key to why fossils are found around the world. It created conditions that would explain how we find fossils of dinosaurs and other creatures all around the world, preserved.

3. Answers will vary — but it is important to note they were created during the Creation Week, were on Noah's ark, and then slowly died out — possibly because of conditions created during the Ice Age after the global Flood. Also note that God called His creation 'good' — supposed millions of years of dinosaur evolution and killing one another would not be considered good.

The New Answers Book 2 — Worksheet Answer Keys

Introduction – Worksheet 1

1. Morality was based on the Bible, and teaching morality from Scripture was common. Prayer and Bible reading were common in public schools. As those things were removed and the Church began to compromise on the authority of Scripture, morality shifted to a secular view. Absolute truth is now rejected by many, even those who claim to be Christians.

2. Showing people that the Bible relates to the real world and that the Bible offers answers for issues that people face every day is a start. The Bible provides everything we need for life and godliness. By standing firm on the truth found in the Bible and proclaiming that truth to a lost world, we can reclaim the culture.

3. Answers will vary.

4. Because he worked to translate the Scriptures into English and get copies of the Bible to the average person. Influenced by Luther and others, Tyndale was an integral part of the Reformation that spread God's written Word throughout the world — particularly to the Western world. At that time, many church leaders believed the Bible should not be in the hands of the common person and that only appointed and scholarly church leaders should tell the public what they should believe. But the spread of God's written Word in the 1500s changed all that as it permeated many nations.

5. Answers will vary.

Chapter 1 – Worksheet 1

1. 1. **Creation**: God created the "very good" earth in six, 24-hour days, approximately 6,000 years ago.
   2. **Corruption**: Adam and Eve ate of the forbidden fruit, bringing sin and death into the world.
   3. **Catastrophe**: God flooded the world to judge a wicked world, but He preserved all who were on the ark.
   4. **Confusion**: God judged rebellious people by confusing their language, and they scattered across the globe.
   5. **Christ**: Jesus Christ, the Creator, came to earth as a man to live a perfect life.
   6. **Cross**: Jesus died on the Cross as a substitute for the penalty of man's sin. He rose again after three days, showing that He conquered death for all who repent and believe.
   7. **Consummation**: The coming time when the Curse will be lifted and God will create a new heaven and earth for believers to enjoy in His presence.

2. One possible answer: The 7 C's provide a way to explain the bad news of sin and present the good news of the gospel.

3. Regardless of age or spiritual maturity level, the 7 Cs provide a way to remember and apply the history found in the Bible to everyday experiences in the world we live in.

4. a) Layers of sedimentary rock in a stream bed.

   Catastrophe — most likely the result of the Flood

   b) The birth of a mule.

   Creation — God created animals to produce after their kind. Horses and donkeys must be of the same biblical kind since they can breed.

   c) Thistles growing along the roadside.

   Corruption — The ground was cursed as a result of Adam's sin; thistles and thorns were part of that curse.

   d) A manger scene outside of a church.

   Creation, Christ — The manger reminds us that the Creator, Jesus Christ, came to earth as a baby to do what the First Adam didn't do — live in complete obedience to God.

   e) An evangelistic crusade at a local arena.

   Corruption, Cross, or Consummation — The reason we must preach repentance toward God is that the first Adam sinned, and all of his descendants are born sinners and willingly disobey God. The solution to sin is the Cross, and those who repent and believe the gospel will spend eternity in God's presence.

f) A rainbow after a storm.

Catastrophe — After the Flood, God used the rainbow as a sign of His covenant to never flood the earth again.

g) Walking through a shopping center and hearing several different languages being spoken.

Confusion — The languages are a result of God confusing the languages at Babel.

h) The beauty of a star-filled sky.

Creation — God created each of the stars on day

i) A nature program showing lions hunting zebras.

Corruption — All death is a result of the fallen world brought about by the sin of man.

j) A disobedient child.

Corruption — All humanity has inherited a sin nature from Adam.

Chapter 2 – Worksheet 1

1. Facts cannot "speak"; they must be interpreted. If we find a smooth, round stone along a stream, do we know that it was a result of natural erosion? No! We can interpret the evidence (smooth, round stone near a stream) in light of our understanding of geologic processes and conclude with a high degree of confidence that it was formed that way. However, there could be other interpretations that are reasonable, especially if new evidence was exposed.

2. A presupposition is something that is assumed to be true without being able to prove it. All reasoning must start from presuppositions, so all people must have presuppositions. Christian reasoning should always start from biblical presuppositions.

3. An analogy related to battling without weapons or armor would be appropriate.

4. Answers will vary by topic.

5. Creationists and evolutionists, Christians and non-Christians, all have the same facts. Think about it: we all have the same earth, the same fossil layers, the same animals and plants, the same stars — the facts are all the same. The difference is in the way we all *interpret* the facts.

Chapter 3 – Worksheet 1

1. The divisive person, according to Scripture, is the one departing from the truth found in the Bible. Romans 16:17–18 and Jude 1:17–19 can be used to validate this position.

2. The teaching of millions of years brought many false teachings into the Church. The acceptance of death before sin, a local Flood, and other teachings began to infiltrate the Church.

3. Jesus would not want us to be divided, but the differences should be based on biblical truths, not religious ideas. In His ministry on the earth, Jesus taught things that caused the listeners to be divided — some believed the biblical position and others rejected it. Truth, by its very nature, creates division. We must stand on the truth of the Bible, even if there are those who disagree.

4. We find the principle of dealing with a divisive person twice and then dismissing them. We need to be careful that we don't lose our effectiveness as evangelists by becoming entangled in prolonged discussions with a person who is not truly interested in learning the truth.

5. Our unity should be in the essential teachings of Scripture and in the person of Jesus Christ.

Chapter 4 – Worksheet 1

1. There have been about 2,000 years between us and Christ, about 2,000 years between Christ and Abraham, and the genealogies in Genesis 5 and 11 show about 2,000 years between Abraham and Adam. This puts the biblical age of the earth at about 6,000 years.

2. The dates range from about 7,500 years (ca. 5501 B.C.) to about 5,800 years (ca. 3836 B.C.) when the Bible is used. Without the Bible, dates have ranged from 7,200 years up to 4.5 billion years.

3. Many different geologists and scientists began thinking in old-age terms, including Werner, Hutton, Lyell, and LaPlace.

4. The biblical age has changed little, but the secular age has increased dramatically over time.

5. No, other methods such as the amount of salt in the ocean, the decay of earth's magnetic field, and the growth of human population indicate

that the earth could not be 4.5 billion years old.

Chapter 5 – Worksheet 1

1. Secular histories, in general, reject the Bible as an authority even though it is the Word of God. Secular histories rely on human reasoning, rather than the Bible, as the authority.

2. Many church leaders, and the Church in general, have compromised the truth of Scripture to fall in line with secular theories. This happened in the 1800s as the idea of millions of years was popularized and added to the Bible. As a result, the absolute authority of Scripture was abandoned. People have realized, in a consistent line of thinking, that if the Bible can't be trusted to give the age of the earth, then Scripture itself cannot be trusted. If the Bible cannot be trusted to teach us of earthly things, why should we trust it on moral issues?

3. Answers will vary.

4. They insist there are gaps in the lists, though they are generally unwilling to point out where those gaps are. Some also accept the secular history, which is based on secular and evolutionary reasoning, and they combine that with the Bible.

5. The Hebrew word *ben* is generally translated as *son* in English. However, other information in the Bible makes it clear that these people are grandsons or more distantly related. So we must take care in interpreting these relationships. The other Hebrew word, *yalad*, does not intend anything other than a father/son relationship in Scripture. "X *begat* Y" always indicates an immediate relationship, but "X is the son of Y" does not necessarily mean an immediate relationship.

Chapter 6 – Worksheet 1

1. Miller's experiment was designed to show how amino acids, the basic building blocks of life, could form by simulating the conditions that were believed to have existed on the early earth.

2. Oxygen is necessary to form the ozone layer, which would have protected evolving life-forms; however, if oxygen were present, it would have destroyed the amino acids that needed to form. So evolutionists must insist that there was no oxygen in the atmosphere, while also claiming that there was oxygen for the ozone layer to form — a fatal paradox.

3. Life could not have evolved in the oceans, in the presence of water, through natural processes. Water, through a process called hydrolysis, breaks the bonds between the amino acids as polypeptides (long chains) begin to form proteins. The proteins would break apart as soon as they began to form.

4. In nature, amino acids are found in two forms, which are mirror images (chirality) of one another. These forms can be thought of like gloves, which are left-handed and right-handed. Proteins in living things contain only left-handed amino acids in their proteins (with very few exceptions). When right-handed amino acids are inserted into the protein chains, the proteins can no longer function properly. No known natural process can explain how proteins would form naturally with only left-handed amino acids.

5. In all known systems, information must originate with an intelligent being. No known natural process can create new information.

6. Evolutionists believe that, given enough time, chance processes can create anything. However, the laws of probability show that it is absurd to believe that an event with a chance of 10-50 will happen. The probability of an average protein forming is 4.9×10^{-191}. The natural formation of life from matter defies the laws of mathematics.

Chapter 7 – Worksheet 1

1. The structure of DNA stores a specific sequence of nucleotides. These nucleotides are represented by the letters A, C, T, and G. The sequence is read in triplets called codons. The sequence ACTTAG would be two codons. Each codon is used to represent an amino acid. A long sequence would be decoded to form a specific protein. This works much like the dots and dashes used in Morse code to represent letters, which are then used to form words.

2.
   1. Point mutation — a single nucleotide changes (ACCGAGCAGTAG).
   2. Inversion mutation — a segment of the nucleotides are reversed (GAGTCACAGTAG).

3. Insertion mutation — a nucleotide is inserted into the sequence (ACTTAGGAGCAGTAG).
4. Deletion mutation — a segment of the nucleotides is lost (ACAGCAGTAG).
5. Frameshift mutation — when an insertion or deletion causes the codons to be read out of sync (ACG,AGC,AGT,AG) or (ACT,CGA,GCA,GTA,G).

3. DNA contains the code that provides the template for assembling the amino acids into the proper sequence to form proteins.
4. In the evolutionary view, mutations are responsible for creating new genetic information which leads to new forms of life. In the biblical view, God created living things; mutations, through the loss of information, have produced much of the variety of life that we see today.
5. From a biblical perspective, we know that Adam and Eve had perfect DNA because God declared all that He had made "very good" (Genesis 1:31). This goes for the original animal and plant kinds as well. They originally had perfect DNA strands with no mistakes or mutations. However, when man sinned against God (Genesis 3), God cursed the ground and the animals, and He sentenced man to die (Genesis 2:17; 3:19). At this time, God seemed to withdraw some of His sustaining power to no longer completely uphold everything in a perfect state. Since then, we would expect mutations to occur and DNA flaws to accumulate. The incredible amount of information that was originally in the DNA has been filtered out, and in many cases lost, due to mutations and natural selection.

Chapter 8 – Worksheet 1

1. Evolutionists assume that apelike creatures evolved into humans, so they interpret the evidence in light of that assumption. Based on the Bible, Christians understand that apelike creatures are not humans and did not evolve into humans. With that knowledge, the evidence is interpreted to support the biblical explanation.
2. Accept any analogy similar to a needle in a haystack or representing a fraction of 1 percent.
3.
   - Apes have larger incisors and canine teeth than humans have.
   - Apes have U-shaped jaws while human jaws are more parabolic.
   - Apes have a much smaller braincase.
   - Ape skulls are slanted from the forehead while human skulls are fairly flat.
   - The eye sockets are not visible from the side in apes, but they are in humans.
   - The leg bones and hipbones of apes are designed to walk on all fours, and the legs of humans are designed for upright walking.
   - The big toes in apes point out while all of the toes are parallel in humans
4. Examples may include Nebraska man, Java man, Lucy, Peking man, or others.
5. The three ways fossils are used to support human evolution are by combining ape and human bones, emphasizing human characteristics of apes, or emphasizing apelike qualities of human fossils.

Chapter 9 – Worksheet 1

1. Isaiah 40:22 and Job 26:10 speak of a spherical earth. Job 26:7 describes the earth suspended in space. Isaiah 40:22 describes the universe expanding as a curtain or tent. All of these have been confirmed by modern science.
2. All of these point to a universe that cannot be billions of years old. The biblical age of 6,000 years is consistent with all of these methods of dating the universe.
3. Primarily, the Bible declares that the universe was supernaturally created by God. However, there are several observations that defy the naturalistic explanations. One example is the model that describes how planets form. Planets that are being discovered around other stars do not make sense in the secular explanations.
4. Answers will vary.
5. Answers will vary, but it needs to attribute Isaiah 40:22 in some way.

Chapter 10 – Worksheet 1

1. In the big bang explanation, all of the mass, energy, and space of the universe were contained

in a singularity. This point rapidly expanded, spreading out the energy and space. The energy eventually formed matter, and then stars and galaxies eventually formed.

2. The Bible describes the earth forming before the stars and moon. The Bible describes plants and dry land being formed before the sun. The Bible describes the earth as being initially covered by water. The Bible describes the supernatural creation of the universe; it does not describe a natural process of creation. The Bible describes a creation in six days, rather than over hundreds of millions of years.

3. Answers may include the missing monopoles, the missing antimatter, the regular expansion of the universe, the addition of the complexity of an inflationary period, and missing stars from the beginning of the universe.

4. If someone truly believed that God used the big bang, he would have to insist that all of the scientists were wrong in rejecting the big bang. By placing his faith in the theories of men, rather than the Bible, the standard of "truth" has changed.

5. Answers will vary.

6. Answers will vary.

Chapter 11 – Worksheet 1

1. The geologic layers that are lowest in the series were deposited first, and the layers that are higher were deposited later.

2. Prior to 1800, the geologic layers were seen as the result of Noah's Flood. The Bible informed the scientific understanding of the day.

3. In general, the uniformitarian view teaches that erosion and deposition happen at a relatively constant rate much as we see them happening today. In other words, looking at the present, we can interpret the past. Catastrophists view the geologic record as the result of successive flood catastrophes on a regional or global scale. However, both views rely on an earth much older than the biblical age.

4. Most of the Church accepted the old-age interpretations and reinterpreted the Bible to accommodate the secular reasoning. The gap theory and various day-age theories resulted from this compromise.

5. A group known as the "scriptural geologists" resisted the old-age interpretations based on philosophical, biblical, and scientific reasoning and relied on Noah's Flood to explain major geologic features.

6. The statement contains several false notions. First, the Bible, rather than secular reasoning, should be used as the authority. Second, a "real geologist" is not defined by his rejection of the Bible. Those who accept the Bible and interpret the rock record in light of Scripture are just as much authorities as those who reject it. It is a logical fallacy to argue that you cannot believe the Bible and be a "real" scientist.

Chapter 12 – Worksheet 1

1. God used the big bang to create the universe; the days of creation were long, overlapping ages; God created new species as others went extinct; nature is as reliable as the Bible; death came before sin; hominids without souls existed before Adam and Eve; and the Genesis Flood was a local event.

2. Progressive creationists view the days in Genesis 1 as vague descriptions of long ages rather than sequential 24-hour days. The "days" were overlapping periods of millions of years during which astronomical and geologic evolution took place.

3. Several points may be made to refute this claim. Romans 8:22 tells us that the whole universe is experiencing the effects of the Curse (Genesis 3). The world we are looking at must be interpreted in light of the fallen state and the entrance of death and sin into the world. We can understand God, in part, by studying His creation, but we cannot make our interpretation of the creation equal to the special revelation of the Bible.

4. Dr. Ross uses these words to describe the Genesis Flood. At first glance, it would seem that he is referring to a flood that covered the entire surface of the earth. However, he actually means a flood that was restricted to a small area.

5. Since the radiometric dating methods are accepted as valid by progressive creationists, and because they believe that Adam and Eve were created about 40,000 years ago, any "humans"

before that time must have been spiritless. This would include Australian Aborigines and Neanderthals.

6. The rainbow promise in Genesis 9:8–17 also makes it clear that the Flood was global. Many regional floods have occurred since Noah's day. If the Flood were a local event, then the rainbow covenant has been broken by God. In Matthew 24:37–39 Jesus compares the coming judgment to the events of the Flood. If the Flood were local, then it follows that the coming judgment will also be local. We know that the judgment is universal.

Chapter 13 – Worksheet 1

1. Paley popularized natural theology and used the analogy of a watchmaker to describe the design in nature. The fact that a watch shows elements of design means that it must have a designer. Likewise, since there is design in nature, nature must be the product of a designer.

2. a) The human eye: It is not necessary; it has specified complexity so it is not a product of chance; there must have been a designer.

   b) A telephone: It is not necessary; it has specified complexity so it is not a product of chance; there must have been a designer.

   c) Paintings found in a cave: The images are not necessary; they have specified complexity and can be interpreted so they are not a product of chance; there must have been a designer.

3. The ID movement does not identify the designer. Individuals are free to choose whichever designer (Brahman, Allah, God, or others) they like. The creator gods of many religious traditions would fit into the ID movement.

4. **Negative**: ID is focused on science, not theology. ID promotes science above Scripture. The identity of the designer is neglected. ID only claims that "certain features" are designed and that the rest evolved. ID promotes that death and disease are natural.

   Positive: The movement has produced many valid scientific discoveries and tools. ID promotes a supernatural explanation for some parts of nature. ID can be used as a way to start conversations about the true Creator.

5. No. While we can understand that God must be a powerful, intelligent being, we cannot understand the details of His plan of salvation. Only through the written Word can we understand God's plan for humanity. We should never divorce the Creator from the Redeemer.

6. According to their own statements, they do not follow any specific religious beliefs. Members of different faiths are involved in the ID movement and research

Chapter 14 – Worksheet 1

1. They teach that everything must be understood in light of evolution and billions of years of earth history.

2. Many scientists and medical practitioners/researchers testify that evolutionary theory played no role in their work. Applying observational science to the present does not depend on understanding the past. There is no need to understand the alleged evolutionary history of the human eye to make glasses or use surgical techniques to correct vision.

3. When we try to explain historical events, we are generally examining evidence that exists in the present. This means that the events themselves cannot be repeated in an experiment. This historical science is not the same as the observational science that produces technology or techniques. Lasers were developed by repeating experiments and refining our understanding of the relationship between matter and energy in the present. Making inferences about the past is not the same as conducting experiments in the present. Historical interpretations will always be influenced by the presuppositions we have.

4. Many scientists, including Newton, Galileo, Maxwell, and Pasteur, could be used as examples of "real" scientists who trusted the Bible. (You can find a list at www.answersingenesis.org/home/area/bios/default.asp.)

5. Statement b is false, as science can never ultimately prove anything. If we attempt to prove that God exists through science, we are placing science — and human reasoning — as authoritative over God. Science is possible

because God made an ordered universe for us to live in. If God had not made the universe, why would we expect it to be logical and orderly? We can expect the future to reflect the past because we trust that God is consistent and He upholds His creation in a consistent way.

6. Answers will vary.

Chapter 15 – Worksheet 1

1. Genesis 5:4 says that Adam and Eve had "other sons and daughters," so Cain likely married a sister or niece.

2. On what do you base your claims of morality? Who has the right to decide what is right or wrong?

3. From Merriam-Webster Online: Pragmatism: an American movement in philosophy founded by C.S. Peirce and William James and marked by the doctrines that the meaning of conceptions is to be sought in their practical bearings, that the function of thought is to guide action, and that truth is preeminently to be tested by the practical consequences of belief. Pragmatists base truth on the experience of individuals, so truth is subject to change and interpretation. Pragmatists generally believe that if it works, it must be true.

   Examples for the last question might include insisting that abortion is wrong because it can harm women, or that gambling is wrong because it causes an increase in thefts. Ultimately, the only standard should be God's standard revealed in the Bible.

4. Pragmatic approaches have no ultimate standard of authority. On the issue of gay marriage, if the argument is used that it spreads HIV, then the argument will fail when a cure for HIV is found.

5. There is really no limit to the types of relationships that could be made legal if society agrees that the laws should be set by majority decision.

6. a) Genesis 2:18–25

   God created a woman, not a man, to complement man.

   b) Leviticus 18:22

   God calls homosexual relations an abomination.

   c) Mark 10:6

   Jesus reaffirms that marriage is between a male and a female.

   d) Romans 1:26–27

   Relations between men and men or women and women are called vile, shameful, and attract a penalty.

   e) 1 Corinthians 6:9–10

   Among the list of unrighteous acts is homosexuality.

   f) 1 Timothy 1:9–10

   Included in the list of things contrary to sound doctrine.

7. Many people have claimed that there is a "gay gene" that predisposes people to be gay. This has not been demonstrated by scientific research. Even if the gene is found, homosexuality is still presented as a sin and must be viewed as such. Sin is sin, regardless of what humans determine is the "cause" of the sin.

8. Unless the Church and the culture return to the authority of Scripture, there is no reason to expect that the sanctity of marriage will be preserved. Ultimately, people need to hear the gospel, repent of their sins, and turn to God.

Chapter 16 – Worksheet 1

1. The biblical records show that life spans decreased dramatically following the Flood.

2. Answers will vary.

3. A genetic bottleneck occurs when a population becomes very small and the amount of genetic variety becomes small. The Flood left eight people to populate the earth, and the confusion at Babel created small language-based groups. Each of these instances would have limited the genetic variety within the population.

4. The cells in our bodies are constantly being replaced, so with only a few exceptions, the cells we were born with are no longer part of our bodies.

5. Answers will vary, but should point to the fact that eternal life can only come from God through repentance and faith in Christ.

Chapter 17 – Worksheet 1

1. The word *canon* means a measuring rod. The Bible is the measure of all things.
2. Several factors, including the exclusion of the writings from the Jewish Scriptures, the fact that they were written during a period when Israel had no prophets, and the way in which they contradict other Scripture are reasons to exclude them from the Bible.
3. The Dead Sea Scrolls confirm the validity of the Old Testament canon and lend support to the accuracy of Old Testament texts.
4. Research will vary.
5. The Pentateuch refers to the first five books of the Bible written by Moses. The Septuagint is a Greek translation of the Old Testament completed in the third century B.C. The Apocrypha is a collection of 14 books that were never considered a part of the Jewish Scriptures but have been included as Scripture by some religious groups.
6. By A.D. 240, Origen was referring to our current set of 27 books as the New Testament.
7. Written books were not common and the letters would have been written on scrolls. A single scroll could not contain all of the text and the information had to be compiled from letters written to churches over a broad region. It simply took time for the leaders to compile the canon into a formal list, and this was only necessary as heretics sought to discredit and twist Scripture.
8. The five basic criteria were having an origin with an Apostle, containing authentic truth, being used from earliest times, acceptance by the churches, and consistency with the rest of Scripture and church teaching.
9. The providence of God in directing the writing, preservation, and compilation of the book we call the Bible.

Chapter 18 – Worksheet 1

1. Physical explanations of the Christmas star include a supernova, a comet, or a conjunction of stars and/or planets that was recognized by the magi.
2. No. God could have used the natural world to mark the birth of Christ, but He could just as easily have used a supernatural marker. The Bible seems to indicate that the magi were aware of the star and Herod was not. The star also led the magi to an individual house — not possible if the star were in the heavens.
3. Since the magi came from the east, and Daniel was in Persia, they may have had access to the Jewish Scriptures, which would have indicated the birth of a king in Israel.
4. Some common misconceptions are the arrival of the magi on the night of Christ's birth, a star visible to everyone, and a star high in the heavens. There are many other examples that are related to facts apart from the star.

Chapter 19 – Worksheet 1

1. The Old Testament names for God used by the Jews are claimed by Jesus Himself and used by other New Testament writers to refer to Him.
2. Only God should receive worship from man, according to passages such as Exodus 34:14 and Matthew 4:10. There are several examples of Jesus accepting worship from men (John 20:28; Matthew 8:2, 9:18) and the angels (Hebrews 1:6). Jesus is worshiped as God because He is, indeed, God.
3. God has revealed that there is one true God, yet we see three persons identified in Scripture and identified as God. If Jesus is not God, then the doctrine of the Trinity, a fundamental doctrine of Christianity, must be rejected. (See the article at www.answersingenesis.org/who-is-god/the-trinity/god-is-triune/ for more scriptural support for the Trinity.)
4. Answers will vary.
5. Answers should include four of the following: eternal, self-existent, every-where present, all-knowing, all-powerful, sovereign, and sinless.

Chapter 20 – Worksheet 1

1. Materialism asserts that mass and energy are all that exist in the universe and that all other supposed entities are fictional.
2. a) Water

   Material, as it is made of matter.

b) Logic

   Nonmaterial, but assumed as true by materialists.

   c) Light

   Material, as it is a form of energy.

   d) Space

   Material, as it is influenced by matter and energy (i.e., it can be bent).

   e) Thoughts

   Nonmaterial.

   f) God

   Nonmaterial, as He is not a natural phenomenon.

   g) Sound

   Material, as it is the transmission of energy through matter.

3. Information can be stored on different media by organizing matter in certain patterns, but it is not part of the matter itself. If you were to weigh a CD before and after storing information on it, the weight would be the same.

4. The Bible contains a coded, symbolically represented message that is intended to cause an action in the reader.

5. Any items with recorded ideas or words would contain information. Items such as staplers, ice cubes, letters on a keyboard, a stereo, etc., show organization but are missing one or more attributes of information.

6. Information is nonmaterial and can be stored on material objects, but it is not a property of the matter it is stored on. The matter can be arranged in a coded, symbolic fashion, but the information is still distinct from the matter itself.

7. Since evolution requires matter to produce new information over time, and matter is not capable of producing nonmaterial entities, evolution must be false.

Chapter 21 – Worksheet 1

1. Historical documents and eyewitness accounts provide the best evidence for the existence of historical figures.

2. We can use observational science to test items from the past that exist in the present, but the conclusions will always be based on assumptions.

3. There is no way to test the events using repeatable experiments, so assumptions must be used to arrive at conclusions about the origin of life. Since there is no historical documentation of the evolutionary position, the assumptions are arbitrary. The Bible gives historical documentation for the origin of life, so the starting assumptions are not arbitrary, but based on God's eyewitness account.

4. There is no documentation for the evolutionary view, while the Bible is God's eyewitness description of the events of the creation of the universe.

5. Because both evolutionary ideals and atheistic ideals are pursued with zeal or conscientious devotion by many, they can be considered religious. Secular humanism, a belief system that espouses atheistic and evolutionary tenets, has been classified as a religion for decades.

6. One reason may be that there is no accountability to a Creator, specifically the God of the Bible. In evolutionary thinking, there is no reason to curb any behaviors — individuals are free to act as they please.

Chapter 22 – Worksheet 1

1. Many recent books and movies have shown people "evidence" that the history of the Bible is false and that recently discovered "truths" prove that the common understanding of the Bible needs to be updated. All of these claims lie on unreliable accounts, documents, and even outright lies portrayed as fact.

2. The ideas are self-contradictory as well as contradictory toward other parts of Scripture.

3. *Extrabiblical* generally refers to any book that is not part of the Bible. The historical writings, gnostic gospels, and religious writings are not considered part of Scripture.

4. Gnostic gospels claimed to be written by Barnabas, Judas, and Mary Magdalene. These books taught a mystical view of nature, dualistic gods, acquiring secret knowledge, a low view of God, and various cult practices.

5. *The Gospel of Philip* suggests that God was

not powerful enough to create the world He desired, and that truth is mystical. *The Gospel of Mary* suggests that Mary Magdalene was Jesus' wife and that they had children. *The Gospel of Barnabas* is used by Muslims to support the claim that Judas died on the cross in Jesus' place and the Messiah was to be descended from Ishmael. *The Gospel of Judas* claims that Judas was given the honorable duty of betraying Christ.

6. Both of these cults believe the Bible is useful, but they change much of the content to fit their beliefs. Other books are elevated above the Bible.

7. Answers may include 2 Timothy 3:16–17; Proverbs 30:5–6; Psalm 19:7–11; and John 17:17.

Chapter 23 – Worksheet 1

1. Uniformitarianism promotes the idea that the actions we see in the present must be used to interpret the past. For example, the rate of erosion we observe today should be used to understand how erosion happened in the past (the present is the key to the past).

2. Most people assume that sedimentary rocks require long ages to form, but that is not the case. By looking at many examples of sedimentary rock forming around modern objects, and other examples, we can conclude that rock can form quite quickly.

3. Observations from Mount Saint Helens and well-preserved fossil fish found in layered rock support the claim that rock layers can form rapidly.

4. Research should show that secular geologists resisted the idea that a flood caused the massive erosion, but later work demonstrated that a megaflood was responsible for the features. PBS even produced a documentary on the issue, though not from a biblical perspective.

5. Organisms must be buried rapidly to prevent them from decaying.

6. These formations are considered to have formed over long ages based on uniformitarian assumptions. However, observational science has demonstrated that the long ages are not necessary.

7. Many appear to be viewing things from a catastrophist viewpoint. Though they still reject a global Flood as described in Genesis, they recognize that the rock layers show rapid burial of organisms.

Chapter 24 – Worksheet 1

1. Many of the rulers reigned at the same time, so adding the length of each individual reign together would create an inflated chronology.

2. The histories must be consistent with the histories of other cultures. If they are not, they must be adjusted to coincide. Ultimately, the Bible should be used as the standard to compare any other history to since it is the account given by God.

3. The Flood would have to be a local flood, or it would have destroyed the pyramids. If the Flood were local, then the people living near the pyramids would not have been destroyed. This would be in direct conflict to the account in Genesis which says all of mankind was destroyed other than those aboard the ark.

4. The revised chronology has shown the consistency of the Egyptian and Israeli histories. Correlation has also been proved between other cultures.

5. Accepting traditional Egyptian chronology necessitates rejection of biblical truth. Accepting biblical chronology allows a reconstruction of ancient chronology on a foundation of truth. Viewing the evidence from a biblical framework makes the histories of Egypt and the Old Testament fit together like two sides of a zipper.

6. Answers will vary.

Chapter 25 – Worksheet 1

1. Other names for Satan include Lucifer, Devil, the accuser, evil one, various dragon and serpent references, Abaddon, prince of the power of the air, Beelzebub, and Belial.

2. There is no specific verse that calls Satan an angel, but he is referred to with angels and as a cherub. He is generally considered a fallen angel, and at least a member of the heavenly host.

3. God created everything in the heavens and the earth (Nehemiah 9:6), so Satan was a created being. Job 38:4–7 seems to indicate that the

angels watched as God created the earth, so it is logical to conclude that Satan and the other heavenly hosts were created on day 1 and at least by day 3. However, there is no explicit passage that states this.

4. If Satan had fallen before God announced everything "very good" on day 6 of creation, God's claim would be false. Since God sanctified the seventh day, it is unlikely that Satan sinned on that day. Adam and Eve were commanded to be fruitful and multiply, so we can conclude they would have attempted to fulfill that command immediately. Since firstborn Cain was obviously a sinner who inherited his sin nature from his parents, the Fall must have happened before he was conceived. Based on these premises, the fall of Satan was probably shortly after the seventh day — at least within the first few weeks before Cain was conceived.

5. The Bible makes it plain that Satan can tempt us but cannot cause us to sin. God does not tempt us to sin, but it is our own desires — our fleshly, sin nature — that lead to sin (James 1:3–15).

6. He will be punished in the lake of fire along with all those who have died in their sins. Many claim that Satan will rule over hell, but that is an unbiblical notion.

7. Those who have repented to God and put their trust in Jesus as Savior will live eternally in heaven. Those who die in their sins will face eternal punishment in hell.

Chapter 26 – Worksheet 1

1. John Scopes was defended by the ACLU lawyer Clarence Darrow, while the State of Tennessee was represented by William Jennings Bryan.

2. The Butler Act was a law passed in Tennessee that made it illegal to teach that man is not the result of divine creation, but that humans had descended from any lower order of animals.

3. Darrow intended to discredit religious fundamentalists in America. Bryan's goals were to let local schools control what is taught and to keep evolution from being taught as a fact.

4. Darrow got Bryan say that God did not create in six days, discrediting the authority of the Bible in the minds of those watching. If the Bible's history cannot be defended as true, then why should its morality be accepted as true? The answer is that there is no consistent reason to reject one and accept the other. If the Bible is truly the Word of God, its authority stands above everything else.

5. We need to provide Bible-based answers to the questions the world asks about the Christian faith. (Who was Cain's wife? Isn't the earth millions of years old? Weren't the days in Genesis 1 long periods of time?) As we do this, people will begin to see that they can trust the Bible when it speaks of "earthly" things, and thus, when it speaks of "heavenly" things (salvation, absolute moral standards, etc.), as Jesus teaches in John 3:12.

Chapter 27 – Worksheet 1

1. Something cannot be yes and no, or true and false, at the same time in the same situation. An apple cannot be both red and green at the same time, though parts of the apple may be red while other parts are green.

2. All of Scripture, both in detail and in its sum, is true, so there cannot be contradictions in the Bible.

3. Only the original autographs would be free of errors since those were the words inspired by God. Minor errors have been introduced by copying manuscripts incorrectly, so the copies we have today can be compared to determine where those mistakes are and how to correct them.

4. Scientific reasoning is based on presuppositions of those making the arguments. The evidence is the same; the interpretations are different because of the presuppositions that inform the conclusions. Simply saying that science is better than the Bible is poor reasoning.

5. The context of a verse informs the reader of the intent of the words used. The Bible plainly states that there is no God (Psalm 14:1). However, reading the verse in context we see that the fool has said in his heart that there is no God. Paul states that all things are lawful (1 Corinthians 6:12) and John says that sin is lawlessness (1 John 3:4). If all things are lawful then nothing is sinful. However, if we read the 1 Corinthians

passage in context, Paul is speaking of eating foods that were forbidden, not transgressing God's moral law.

6. Since we are looking at a translation of Hebrew, Greek, and Aramaic into English, there can never be a perfect translation of the ideas. Using multiple translations can help us correct misunderstandings. Another problem is that language changes and current translations may correct those misunderstandings found in earlier translations.

7. If we do not accept that words change in meaning, we may read a text and understand it to mean the complete opposite of what the author intended. "Prevent" used to mean to come before, while today it means to block an action. Reading Psalm 88:13 in the KJV with a modern understanding of the word "prevent" would likely lead us to a wrong conclusion about the verse.

8. Because we can compare manuscripts of different ages, we can determine likely insertions and deletions due to copyist errors. This does not mean that the Bible contains errors and should not be trusted, but that the errors are so rare and identifiable that they are insignificant.

Chapter 28 – Worksheet 1

1. The extrabiblical reference of Peleg confirms the biblical account and also links it to the events of Babel.

2. Many civilizations have similar buildings, known as ziggurats. It is suggested that the Tower of Babel was probably a ziggurat. As people spread across the globe, they carried this idea with them and constructed similar structures where they settled.

3. Many genealogies can be traced back to the sons and grandsons of Noah, or Noah himself. Some of the names are in derived forms, but are present in many cultures. This confirms the accuracy of the accounts in the Bible.

4. Cush is still used for the Ethiopians, the Aramaic language comes from Aram, the Hebrew nation draws its name form Eber, Ashkenaz is the Hebrew name for Germany, Madai was the namesake of the Medes, and many other examples.

5. Linguists have grouped languages into about 100 language families. All of the languages within a family share common features that can be traced back through time to a distinct source. These language families are likely the result of the languages created at Babel.

Chapter 29 – Worksheet 1

1. The three basic positions are at the time of fertilization (conception), at the time of implantation into the womb, or at the time of birth or when the umbilical cord is cut. However, there are many variations on these positions.

2. Fertilization occurs when the egg and the sperm unite. This single cell then begins to divide and moves to the womb, where it implants in the wall as a blastocyst. The process of development continues through many more stages until the baby is born.

3. The meaning of conception has changed from the time of fertilization to the time of implantation in medical usage. If we say life begins at conception, it may be misconstrued as implantation when we mean fertilization. Defining the terms is important in discussions, especially over potentially contentious ideas.

4. Answers will vary.

5. The Bible is always a reliable source on any issue in our lives, especially those with moral implications.

6. The biblical language of those in the womb is always of a living person, never a fetus or anything else.

7. The most obvious issue is abortion, but the issue is also linked to the stem cell debate, cloning, birth control methods, and ultimately the authority of Scripture over man's reasoning.

Chapter 30 – Worksheet 1

1. Good science involves a systematic approach to studying a topic, generally referred to as the scientific method. This method develops hypotheses that can be tested in observable, repeatable experiments in order to affirm or refute the hypothesis leading to further study.

2. Science can prove things false under certain

conditions, but it can never ultimately prove anything to be true. We can do experiments to demonstrate how objects behave under different circumstances, but we can never say with certainty, based on past experiments, that they will always behave that way or that new evidence will lead to a better understanding.

3. The physical behaviors that Newton described worked well for objects in our everyday experience but failed to explain how atomic and subatomic particles behave. Quantum mechanics and relativity theory were developed to explain the physics of these objects where Newton's laws failed.

4. Einstein showed that space and time are actually a fourth dimension that can be altered by mass and energy. He also showed that space can bend and flow, and that time can pass at different rates in different conditions — all ideas contrary to earlier notions and theories.

5. While quantum mechanics and relativity have been demonstrated to be valid through prediction and experimentation, string theory has no experimental basis. Scientists are still trying to test the hypotheses associated with string theory using particle accelerators and other techniques.

Chapter 31 – Worksheet 1

1. Only that they were buried at the same time, not that they lived together.

2. Many evolutionists claim that the extinction of dinosaurs and other creatures recorded in the rock record is associated with a chemical layer that could have come from an asteroid. From a biblical perspective, the volcanic activity associated with the Flood can explain the layer as well. The Flood is the explanation for the extinction of most of the life on earth — all land creatures not aboard the ark.

3. We see specific communities of organisms in zones on the earth today. If there were a global flood today, the animals that live in the high desert would not be buried with animals that live in coastal communities. Likewise, during the Genesis Flood, certain areas would have been flooded and buried before others. While there would be some mixing of organisms in adjacent zones, we would expect to find organisms from lower zones lower in the rock record and those from higher zones higher in the rock record.

4. Sea creatures would have been buried first as the fountains of the great deep broke open. Creatures such as worms, brachiopods, and bivalves would have no way to escape the debris stirred up and carried by currents onto the continental shelves.

5. The size, shape, and density of the organisms will determine what layer they are deposited in if they are in a flowing mass of mud. Very dense and streamlined organisms would settle to the bottom of the flow while less dense organisms would move or remain on top. This sorting action could account for much of the orientation of organisms in the rock record.

6. Vertebrates, to different degrees, are very mobile, instinctively flee danger, and struggle to survive. All of these factors combined can explain much about the order of organisms in the rock record. Fish would likely be found higher than shellfish and mammals higher than amphibians in the event of a global flood.

Conclusion – Worksheet 1

1. Understanding that the Bible presents a logical faith, not a blind one, is important. By studying Scripture we can come to a proper understanding of the creation and other issues. But the most important thing revealed in Scripture is God's plan of salvation through the gospel.

2. Answers will vary.

The New Answers Book 1&2 — Practical Test Answer Key

Practical Test 1

1. abiogenesis
2. adaptation
3. adaptive radiation
4. anthropology
5. Archaeopteryx
6. artifact
7. atheism
8. Australopithecus
9. beneficial mutation
10. biblical creation model
11. big-bang model
12. catastrophism
13. cell theory
14. compromise
15. created kind (baramin)
16. Cro-Magnon man
17. Darwinism
18. day-age theory
19. deism
20. eisegesis
21. exegesis
22. mold and cast
23. permineralized
24. framework hypothesis
25. gap theory
26. gene pool
27. half-life
28. historical (origins) science
29. hominid
30. *Homo erectus*
31. *Homo habilis*
32. *Homo sapiens*
33. humanism
34. Java man
35. Kennewick man
36. life (biological)
37. macroevolution
38. microevolution
39. mitochondrial Eve
40. natural selection
41. Neanderthal/Neandertal
42. neo-Darwinism
43. old-earth creation
44. operational (observational) science
45. uniformitarian model
46. catastrophic model
47. progressive creation
48. punctuated equilibrium
49. speciation
50. spontaneous generation
51. theistic evolution
52. theory
53. transitions/transitional forms
54. uniformitarianism
55. *Yom*

Practical Test 2

1. Answers will vary.
2. Answers will vary.
3. Answers will vary.
4. Answers will vary.
5. The word *science* in English comes from a Latin word, *scientia*, which means knowledge.

    An interesting fact is that in the Old and New testaments, "science" and "knowledge" translate the same Greek and Hebrew words respectively! (www.icr.org/article/science-true-false/)

Practical Test 3

1. Pontius Pilate killed Christus (Christ) and a few years later, Nero publicly persecuted the

Christians in cruel and horrible ways. Christians were not creating violence in the city but they were punished anyway. Many non-Christians felt compassion for those persecuted because of Nero's dislike of them.

2. There are laws in the United States and many other countries for religious freedom; we are not an empire ruled by one man, but a republic representative of the people. Many other governments are democracies as well. While some government policies may try to impede religious freedom, the courts often helped to balance out and preserve religious rights. Yes, religious rights in some ways are under attack, but the method of punishments are fines, rather than tortures and death.

3. Answers will vary but should note that Josephus was kinder and more complimentary in his tone, and make it clear that the decision against Jesus was a political one more than a legal one.

4. Answers will vary but should include examples — while Josephus describes many of the attributes and popular feelings about Christ, he does not identify Him as the Son of God. He does note He was killed and appeared alive after three days as was foretold much as the Scripture describes.

5. He is noted as being the brother of James and as also having been called Christ.

6. Answers will vary. Knowing that Jesus was a real figure in history shows again that the Bible is accurate in its recording of history and the life and death of Jesus. Other sources are not needed to prove the Bible, but are evidence again of its accuracy.

Practical Test 4

1. Answers will vary. If there is "design" then we cannot be one of billions of random, accidental processes that created the universe, the world, us, and all life that we know about. If we are then products of deliberate design, who did it — and why — are the next two natural questions. Read Romans 1:20–21: *For since the creation of the world His invisible attributes are clearly seen, being understood by the things that are made, even His eternal power and Godhead, so that they are without excuse, because, although they knew God, they did not glorify Him as God, nor were thankful, but became futile in their thoughts, and their foolish hearts were darkened.*

2. Answers will vary. They agree that there is obvious design to be found, but there is no consensus on "who" did it — some may think it is an alien race, others might think it is God — but by not identifying the designer, they can avoid crediting God or aliens or whomever they feel may have done it. All of that takes people away from the truth of God's Word as found in Genesis.

3. Answers will vary. There are some Christians involved in the intelligent design movement. By suggesting there is a designer, this means many critics automatically assume that this is the God of the Bible and just a way of getting religion or unscientific ideas into classrooms or textbooks. But again, if God is not identified as the designer, then it is not a biblically accurate concept and doesn't uphold the authority of Scripture over man-made theories.

4. Answers will vary. Because you are simply acknowledging there is design — not giving credit to the Designer and His plan for mankind. By noting design, we acknowledge nature, not God and His love for us.

Practical Test 5

1. Answers will vary.
2. Answers will vary.

Practical Test 6

1. Answers will vary, but it needs to note that we, on our own, cannot save ourselves from the sin in our lives. We are powerless to save ourselves and so we must have a Savior.

2. Answers will vary, but we have to admit we are sinners — as we are, we cannot be saved because of this sin, and we want to be forgiven and have salvation.

3. Answers will vary, but God has given us the only path to salvation in the form of Jesus Christ, His Son, as the perfect sacrifice for our sin.

4. Answers will vary, but it is important that by acknowledging our need for a Savior and receiving Christ we are choosing to follow Him and His Word, and letting this be the guiding principle of our lives.

5. Answers will vary. There is no way to buy or earn the gift of salvation — it is freely given by Christ to those who receive Him as their Lord and Savior. It is waiting for those who have yet to receive it. When you receive it, you are acknowledging Him in your heart, and His importance in your life.

6. Sinner's Prayer: Prayers will vary.

Practical Test 7

Answers will vary on the complete Practical Test.

Practical Test 8

1. They are — behemoth has attributes of animals that we today call dinosaurs and although not considered a dinosaur because they are land animals, leviathan is also mentioned, which was some kind of very powerful sea reptile. Remember the word *dinosaur* was not even invented until the 1800s — long after the Bible was written, but the word *dragon* is another word some feel is used to describe dinosaurs in the Bible.

2. They didn't need to — remember the biblical word *kinds* — it doesn't say take each and every animal, it said two of each kind were taken — and these would include dinosaurs. Remember, kinds and species are not exactly the same. There are more species than kinds — these are just different ways of categorizing the same animals. As for their size, remember, nothing says they had to be adult members of kind — so juveniles may have been on the ark instead.

3. Yes. All scientists — secular and creationist — are looking at the same evidence. But they have different starting points. Secularists see the features of the world having been the product of long periods of geologic activity over time, though some are now more receptive to the concept of catastrophic forces being able to quickly make changes to the earth's surface.

4. Mount St. Helens in the early 1980s provided an important window into these processes and how quickly the landscape can be dramatically altered due to catastrophic processes.

5. The scientific data is not faulty; it is their interpretation of it that is faulty. And yes, many scientists are reluctant to cede any point that give validity to the concept of the Bible being true, and there being a supernatural power, God, that created the natural world.

Essay questions: Essays will vary on both questions.

The New Answers Book 1 & 2 — Semester Test Answer Key

Semester Test 1

1. Logical reasoning and scientific inquiry are only possible in a world created by a logical and scientific Creator. God is self-consistent; He does not contradict Himself. The world He created would then naturally also follow logical and consistent laws. If the world was the result of mutations and chance, random processes, there is no foundation for logic or scientific laws. The very nature of logic comes from the logical and orderly character of its Creator.

2. Man's fallible opinion allows for millions of years of earth history, but this opinion is strictly that — opinion. Essential to God's character is holiness. He cannot lie, and He cannot deceive. His Word is clear in its teaching. To say that God used evolution in His creation is adding words and ideas of fallible man to the infallible words of God.

3. All allow for millions of years of death, disease, and suffering to take place before Adam sinned. All allow fallible theories of scientists to determine the meaning of Scripture. GT accepts that the six days were normal-length days; PC/TE tries to twist the days into representing long ages. GT opposes evolution, TE accepts evolutionary processes (albeit, God-directed).

4. God's Laws, biological deformities, etc.; wording may vary but need to touch on these concepts.

5. The intelligence and physical strength of the people of Noah's day were likely at least equal to, if not superior to, ours today. There is no reason why Noah and his sons couldn't have built the ark on their own. They also could have hired skilled laborers to help build the ark. Also, keep in mind that these people were not primitive in any way. Their tools, machines, and building techniques were completely sufficient and effective to build such a huge vessel.

6. The earth's terrain, from canyons and craters to coal beds and caverns, indicates a catastrophic history. Layers of strata show that they were laid down by water, and fossils buried in these layers give evidence to an extremely rapid burial.

7. If we accept God's Word, beginning with Genesis, as being true and authoritative, then we can explain dinosaurs and make sense of the evidence we observe in the world around us. In doing this, we are helping people see that Genesis is absolutely trustworthy and logically defensible, and is what it claims to be — the true account of the history of the universe and mankind. And what one believes concerning the Book of Genesis will ultimately determine what one believes about the rest of the Bible. This, in turn, will affect how a person views him or herself, and fellow human beings, and what life is all about, including their need for salvation.

8. One of the biggest justifications for racial discrimination in modern times is the belief that people groups have evolved separately. Thus, different groups are at allegedly different stages of evolution, and so some people groups are more backward than others. Therefore, the other person may not be as fully human as you.

9. Natural selection, according to evolutionists, is defined as evolutionary change or the driving force behind evolutionary change. According to creationists, natural selection is the process whereby organisms with certain characteristics survive better in a given environment or under a given selective pressure.

10. Since evolution places death before Adam and Eve sinned in the Garden of Eden, death has always existed and impacted the earth and mankind. There is no beginning of it, and there is no ending to it. Man is simply the end result of millions of years of death and suffering. With this belief system as one's foundation, there is no future hope for mankind.

Semester Test 2

1. Showing people that the Bible relates to the real world and that the Bible offers answers for issues that people face every day is a start. The Bible provides everything we need for life and godliness. By standing firm on the truth found in the Bible and proclaiming that truth to a lost world, we can reclaim the culture.

2. A presupposition is something that is assumed to be true without being able to prove it. All reasoning must start from presuppositions, so all people must have presuppositions. Christian reasoning should always start from biblical presuppositions.

3. There have been about 2,000 years between us and Christ, about 2,000 years between Christ and Abraham, and the genealogies in Genesis 5 and 11 show about 2,000 years between Abraham and Adam. This puts the biblical age of the earth at about 6,000 years.

4. From a biblical perspective, we know that Adam and Eve had perfect DNA because God declared all that He had made "very good" (Genesis 1:31). This goes for the original animal and plant kinds as well. They originally had perfect DNA strands with no mistakes or mutations. However, when man sinned against God (Genesis 3), God cursed the ground and the animals, and He sentenced man to die (Genesis 2:17, 3:19). At this time, God seemed to withdraw some of His sustaining power to no longer completely uphold everything in a perfect state. Since then, we would expect mutations to occur and DNA flaws to accumulate. The incredible amount of information that was originally in the DNA has been filtered out, and in many cases lost, due to mutations and natural selection.

5. Evolutionists assume that apelike creatures evolved into humans, so they interpret the evidence in light of that assumption. Based on the Bible, Christians understand that apelike creatures are not humans and did not evolve into humans. With that knowledge, the evidence is interpreted to support the biblical explanation

6. The Bible describes the earth forming before the stars and moon. The Bible describes plants and dry land being formed before the sun. The Bible describes the earth as being initially covered by water. The Bible describes the supernatural creation of the universe; it does not describe a natural process of creation. The Bible describes a creation in six days, rather than over hundreds of millions of years.

7. In general, the uniformitarian view teaches that erosion and deposition happen at a relatively constant rate, much as we see them happening today. In other words, looking at the present, we can interpret the past. Catastrophists view the geologic record as the result of successive flood catastrophes on a regional or global scale. However, both views rely on an earth much older than the biblical age.

8. Statement b is false, as science can never ultimately prove anything. If we attempt to prove that God exists through science, we are placing science — and human reasoning — as authoritative over God. Science is possible because God made an ordered universe for us to live in. If God had not made the universe, why would we expect it to be logical and orderly? We can expect the future to reflect the past because we trust that God is consistent and He upholds His creation in a consistent way.

9. One reason may be that there is no accountability to a Creator, specifically the God of the Bible. In evolutionary thinking, there is no reason to curb any behaviors — individuals are free to act as they please.

10. The Bible makes it plain that Satan can tempt us but cannot cause us to sin. God does not tempt us to sin, but it is our own desires — our fleshly, sin nature — that lead to sin (James 1:3–15).

11. Since we are looking at a translation of Hebrew, Greek, and Aramaic into English, there can never be a perfect translation of the ideas. Using multiple translations can help us correct misunderstandings. Another problem is that language changes and current translations may correct those misunderstandings found in earlier translations.

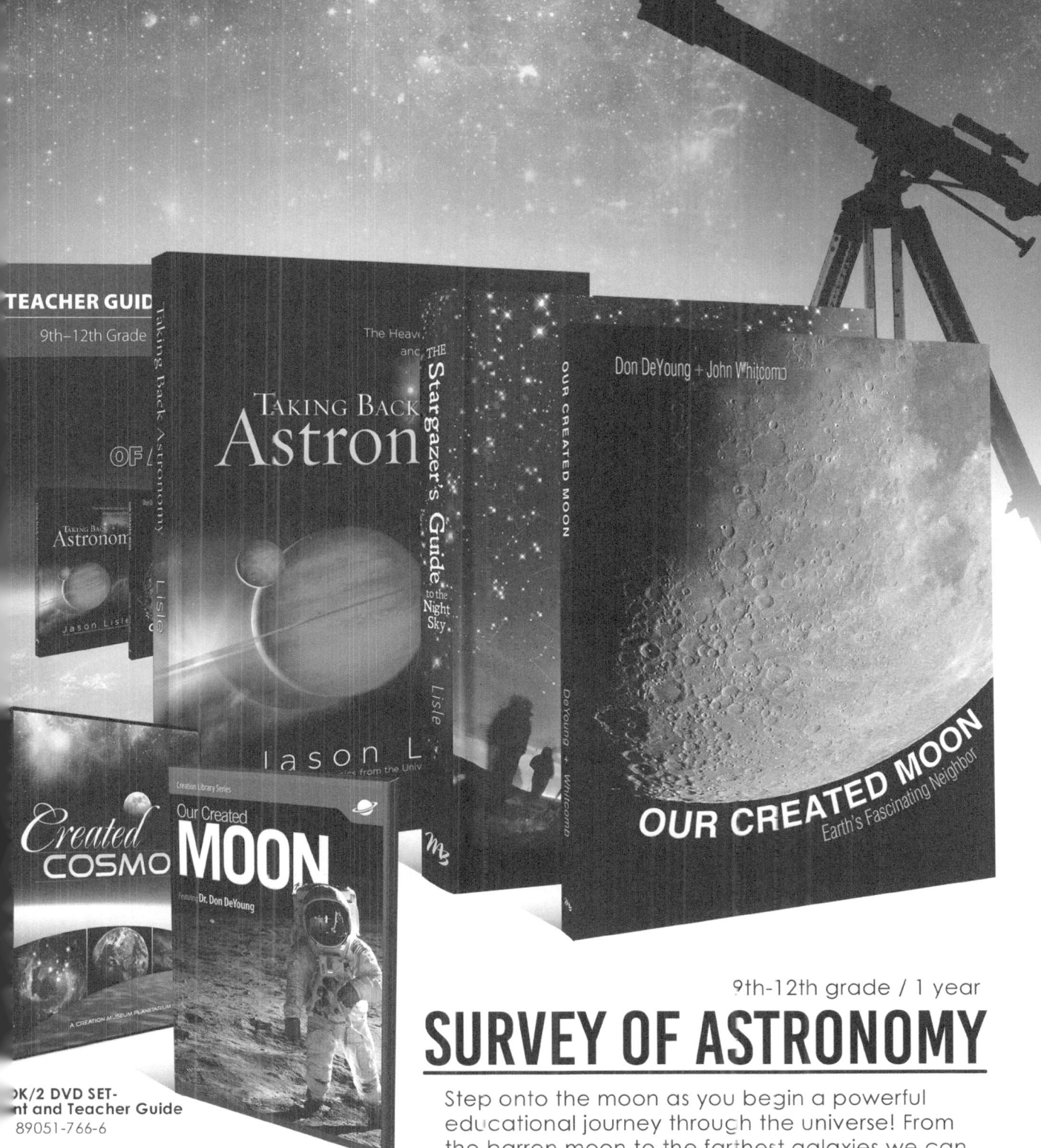

9th-12th grade / 1 year

SURVEY OF ASTRONOMY

Step onto the moon as you begin a powerful educational journey through the universe! From the barren moon to the farthest galaxies we can see, you will learn about the facts and wonders of this marvel of creation. Teams solid science with a biblical perspective to answer important questions about the stars, planets, and the place of Earth in this vast expanse!

AVAILABLE AT MasterBooks.com & OTHER PLACES WHERE FINE BOOKS ARE SOLD.

Daily Lesson Plan

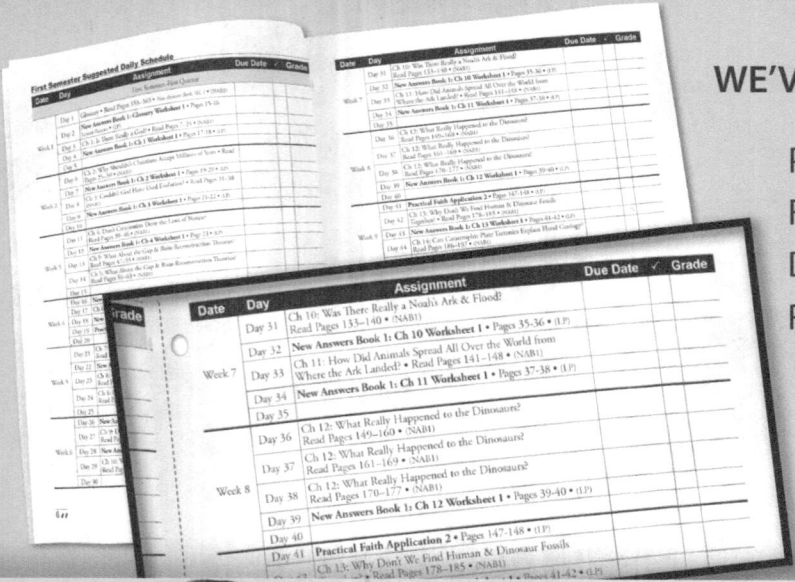

WE'VE DONE THE WORK FOR YOU!

PERFORATED & 3-HOLE PUNCHED
FLEXIBLE 180-DAY SCHEDULE
DAILY LIST OF ACTIVITIES
RECORD KEEPING

"THE TEACHER GUIDE MAKES TH
SO MUCH EASIER AND TAKES
GUESS WORK OUT OF IT FOR

HOMESCHOOL

Master Books® Homeschool Curricul

Faith-Building Books & Resources
Parent-Friendly Lesson Plans
Biblically-Based Worldview
Affordably Priced

Master Books® is the leading publisher of books and resources based upon a Biblical worldview that points to God as our Creator.